SAGE LEADERSHIP

Also by Thomas Cleary

The Art of War, by Sun Tzu

Awakening to the Tao, by Liu I-ming

The Book of Five Rings, by Miyamoto Musashi

I Ching: The Book of Change

The Japanese Art of War:
Understanding the Culture of Strategy

Mastering the Art of War, by Zhuge Liang & Liu Ji

Pocket Taoist Wisdom

Taoist Meditation:
Methods for Cultivating a Healthy Mind and Body

Training the Samurai Mind: A Bushido Sourcebook

Ways of Warriors, Codes of Kings:
Lessons in Leadership from the Chinese Classics

The Way of the World:
Readings in Chinese Philosophy

Wen-tzu: Understanding the Mysteries, by Lao-tzu

Zen Lessons: The Art of Leadership

SAGE LEADERSHIP

Taoist Wisdom to
Overcome Conflict and
Create a Just World

TRANSLATIONS FROM THE
HUAINANZI

Thomas Cleary

SHAMBHALA

Shambhala Publications, Inc.
2129 13th Street
Boulder, Colorado 80302
www.shambhala.com

Cover art: *Autumn Landscape*, leaf from *Album for Zhou Lianggong*,
Xiang Shengmo, 1654, Seymour Fund, 1964.
Cover design: Daniel Urban-Brown
Interior design: Greta D. Sibley

9 8 7 6 5 4 3 2 1

Printed in the United States of America

Shambhala Publications makes every effort to
print on acid-free, recycled paper.

Shambhala Publications is distributed worldwide by
Penguin Random House, Inc., and its subsidiaries.

LIBRARY OF CONGRESS CATALOGING-IN-PUBLICATION DATA

Names: Cleary, Thomas F., 1949–2021, translator, editor.
Title: Sage leadership: Taoist wisdom to overcome conflict
and create a just world / Thomas Cleary.
Other titles: Huainan zi. Selections. English.
Description: Boulder, Colorado: Shambhala, 2022.|
"This book was previously published under the title
The Book of Leadership and Strategy"—Colophon.
Identifiers: LCCN 2022010947 | ISBN 9781611809763 (trade paperback)
Classification: LCC BL1900.H83 E5 2022 | DDC 181/.114—dc23/eng20220518
LC record available at https://lccn.loc.gov/2022010947

Contents

vii   Translator's Introduction

1   On State and Society

59   On Warfare

77   On Peace

113   On Wisdom

Translator's Introduction

This book is a collection of extracts from *Huainanzi*, "The Masters of Huainan," an early Taoist classic following the ancient tradition of Lao-tzu and Chuang-tzu. Composed over two thousand years ago, *Huainanzi* is one of the oldest and most prestigious works of Taoist philosophy.

The book of the masters of Huainan is a record of sayings on civilization, culture, and government. More detailed and explicit than either of its great forerunners, Lao-tzu's *Tao-te Ching*, and the *Chuang-tzu*, it embraces the full range of natural, social, and spiritual sciences encompassed in classical Taoism. It links environmental husbandry, personal development, and sociopolitical evolution into a comprehensive vision of human life.

The origin of the book of the Huainan masters is traced to an inner circle of Taoist sages at the court of the king of Huainan, ruler of a small principality within the vast empire of Han dynasty China in the second century B.C.E. The king of Huainan was a distinguished patron of learning, and his court was already a flourishing center of culture when a group of eight Taoist masters appeared with these teachings.

Although the ideas of the masters of Huainan are based on the famous Taoist classics by Lao-tzu and Chuang-tzu, their emphasis differs in one important respect. The works of Lao-tzu and Chuang-tzu are products of China's era of the Warring States, and their attitudes toward involvement in the world reflect the corruption and turmoil of their times. The Huainan masters, in contrast, lived in a time of national reconstruction following the end of centuries of civil war; their teachings are thus more positive and constructive than those of the wartime Taoists.

The selections from the book of the Huainan masters translated here focus on the core principles of their teachings. Like other Taoist classics, these writings are for contemplation and not indoctrination; therefore they do not follow a rigid system of dogma. In order to facilitate absorption by a modern audience, these extracts have been grouped into four sections: state and society, warfare, peace, and wisdom. Being Taoist teachings, these four groups of meditations are linked to one another like the four seasons of a year.

The Huainan masters' teachings on government deal with a broad range of elements composing the fabric of state and society, including organization and human relations, economy, education, culture, customs and morals, industry, and husbandry.

The masters advocate a pluralistic yet egalitarian society with minimal government interference and maximum opportunity for individual fulfillment. They also propose a conscious balance between the human and natural worlds, regarding it as so necessary that they refer to this balance itself as divine.

The ideals of the Taoist group are graphically illustrated by their comparisons between what they view as progressive, evolutionary societies and what they consider degenerate, decadent societies. These sketches also symbolize different phases in the development of individual human consciousness.

The Huainan masters speak of healthy societies in terms of balance and harmony on each level of being, from the way the individual human body-mind complex experiences itself to the way it experiences interaction with the natural and social worlds.

Degenerate societies, in contrast, are characterized by extreme exaggeration of some human capacities and corresponding atrophy of others, in both individual and collective life. The Huainan masters observe this phenomenon in terms of cause and effect as indicative of countercause and countereffect, leading to the idea of liberation.

The two main factors in human psychology pictured by the Huainan masters as most destructive are greed and aggression. These are connected to fear and blindness, and all together they produce conflict and violence. Warfare is one of the paradoxical symbols of ancient Taoism, being the epitome of conflict and violence but also representing a way of ending conflict and violence, a symbol of self-purification.

All of the original classics of Taoism contain teachings on the causes and effects of warfare; the book of the Huainan masters is foremost among them in scope and detail, distilling the essences of the *I Ching*, Lao-tzu's *Tao-te Ching*, the *Chuang-tzu*, and Sun-tzu's classic on strategy and tactics, *The Art of War*. These teachings all have literal meanings in the context of group interactions and symbolic meanings in the context of the individual relationship to the self.

Being principally concerned with logical ethics in their sayings on warfare, the Huainan masters also deal with larger questions of sociopolitical morale in terms of its relations to conflict and reconciliation. Thus the masters define their conceptions of just and unjust wars in parallel with their comparisons between progressive and repressive societies and between balanced and exaggerated individuals. Harmony among persons and peoples is envisioned as arising from harmony within the self and with nature itself.

The teachings of the Huainan masters on harmony and peace turn to the concerns of the individual human being—the fundamental unit of the family, society, and state. Although ancient Taoists considered the harmony of the individual with the universe to be an originally natural condition, they believed it was already inaccessible to the average person without special means of recovering it.

In the Huainan masters' teachings on peace are contained the foundations of what later came to be called the science of essence and life, or the way of spiritual alchemy. This is the individual inner teaching of Taoism on grooming the "three treasures" of vitality, energy, and spirit.

The masters present a wide variety of techniques for this process of enhancement, from ways of managing time, handling resources, and establishing priorities, to ways of attaining deep rest and peace of mind. These Taoist arts of living are held to be capable of producing an evolutionary change in the individual, resulting in what classics call the complete person, the real human being, or the sage.

The final selection of extracts from the teachings of the Huainan masters translated here deals with the inner and outer life of Taoist sages, the means and ends of Taoist wisdom. In these sayings the Huainan masters outline the ways by which the ancient Taoist illuminates attained their knowledge, sustained their well-being, and realized their freedom.

SAGE LEADERSHIP

On State and Society

Very great leaders in their domains are only
   known to exist.
Those next best are beloved and praised.
The lesser are feared and despised.

—Lao-tzu, *Tao-te Ching*

When society is orderly, a fool alone cannot disturb it; when society is chaotic, a sage alone cannot bring order.

—

To blame the Tao for not working while we are living in a polluted world is like tying down a unicorn from two directions and expecting it to run a thousand miles.

Place a monkey in a cage, and it is the same as a pig, not because it isn't clever and quick, but because it has no place to freely exercise its capabilities.

—

Even wise leaders must await appropriate circumstances. Appropriate circumstances can only be found at the right time and cannot be fulfilled through being sought by knowledge.

—

The wise leave the road and find the Way; fools cling to the Way and lose the road.

—

The basic task of government is to make the populace secure. The security of the populace is based on meeting needs. The basis of meeting needs is in not depriving people of their time. The basis of not depriving people of their time is in minimizing government exactions and expenditures. The basis of minimizing government exactions and expenditures is moderation of desire. The basis of moderating desire is in returning to essential nature. The basis of returning to essential nature is in removing the burden of accretions.

Remove the burden of accretions, and there is openness. To be open is to be equanimous. Equanimity is a basic element of the Way; openness is the house of the Way.

—

Those who can become rulers must be able to find winners. Those who can win over opponents must be strong. Those who can be strong are able to use the power of other people. To be able to use the power of other people, it is necessary to win people's hearts. To be able to win people's hearts, it is necessary to have self-mastery. To be capable of self-mastery, it is necessary to be flexible.

—

The ancient establishment of rulers was not for the service of their desires; and when sages lived in lowly positions it was not for the purpose of taking things easy.

Rulership was set up because the strong oppressed the weak, the many did violence to the few, the cunning fooled the simple, the bold attacked the timid, people kept knowledge to themselves and did not teach, people accumulated wealth and did not share it. So the institution of rulership was set up to equalize and unify them.

—

Sages do not consider mountains high or rivers wide when they take on the embarrassment and disgrace of dealing with political leaders. This is not because of greed for emolument or desire for rank; it is because they want to serve the interests of the world and get rid of what is harmful to the people.

Traditions about sage kings of old as recorded in ancient documents say that Shennong was haggard, Yao was emaciated, Shun was burnt black, Yu was calloused. Looking at these enlightened leaders of old, we can see that sages do worry and toil for the common people very much indeed.

—

When people are influenced by their rulers, they follow what the rulers do, not what they say.

—

When laws are set up and a system of rewards is established, yet this cannot change the mores of the people, it is because this does not work without sincerity.

—

Spiritual government is the very best. Next best is to make it impossible for people to do wrong. Next after that is to reward the worthy and punish the disruptive.

—

As a balance scale is fair insofar as it weighs things impartially and a plumb line is correct insofar as it determines straight lines impartially, a ruler who applies the law without personal likes and dislikes can thereby command.

—

What restrains and punishes is law. When people have been punished and yet are not resentful, this is called the Way. When the Way prevails, people have no politics.

—

In ancient times, those who gave rewards well could encourage people at little cost. Those who punished well prevented treachery with minimal penalties. Those who gave well were frugal in expenditures yet were charitable. Those who took well had much income yet were not resented by anyone.

—

Punishments and penalties are not enough to change habits; executions and massacres are not enough to prevent treachery. Only spiritual influence is valuable.

—

Strict laws and harsh punishments are not the work of ruling kings.

—

In ancient times, under sage leadership, the laws were liberal and penalties easygoing. The prisons were empty, everyone had the same mores, and no one was treacherous.

Government in later times was not like this. Those above were rapacious beyond measure, while those below were covetous and inconsiderate. The common people were poor and miserable, and they fought with each other. They worked hard but did not achieve anything. Clever deceivers appeared, and there came to be many thieves and robbers.

Superiors and subordinates resented each other, directives were not carried out, and officers of the government did not strive to return to the Tao. Heedless of the fundamental, the officers attended to trivialities; lessening rewards, they increased punishments. As they tried to govern in this way, disorder increased.

———

Many intellectuals in society have departed from the root of the Way and its power; they say manners and duties are sufficient to govern the world. It is not possible to talk to them about the arts of leadership.

———

When rulers are very crafty, their subjects are very devious. When rulers have many obsessions and interests, their subjects do a lot of posturing. When rulers are uneasy, their subjects are unsettled. When rulers are very demanding, their subjects are contentious. If you don't straighten this out at the root but concern yourself with the branches, this is like stirring up dust as you try to clean a room, like carrying a bunch of kindling as you try to put out a fire.

Therefore, the affairs of sages are limited and easy to manage; their requirements are few and easy to satisfy. They are benevolent without trying; they are trusted without speaking; they gain without seeking; they succeed without striving. They perceive reality alone, embrace virtue, and extend sincerity. Everyone follows them like echoes of sound, like reflections of form. What they cultivate is fundamental.

—

When political leaders ruin their countries and wreck their lands, themselves to die at others' hands, a laughingstock of all the world, it is always because of their desires.

—

In ancient times, governments required little and people had enough. The rulers were benevolent and their ministers were loyal. Parents were kind and children were obedient. Everyone acted lovingly, and there was no resentment among them.

—

In ancient wars, they did not kill the young or capture the old; but what was considered just in antiquity is now considered ludicrous. What was considered honorable in ancient times is now considered shameful. What made for order in ancient times now makes for chaos.

Chieftains of high antiquity did not administer rewards or punishments, yet the people did not do wrong. But those who set up governments now are unable to dispense with law to govern the people. One ancient leader subdued unruly tribes just by performing a martial dance; but those who carry out police actions now cannot control the strong and violent without arms.

—

In the space of one generation, the cultural and the martial may shift in relative significance, insofar as there are times when each is useful. Nowadays, however, martialists repudiate culture, and the cultured repudiate the martial. Adherents of cultural and martial arts reject each other, not knowing their functions according to the time.

—

Human abilities are not sufficient to be relied on alone; the arts of the Way are to be carried out in public. The laws of a dysfunctional society make measures high and punish those who do not reach; they make responsibilities heavy and penalize those who cannot bear them; they make difficulties dangerous and execute those who cannot face them.

When the people are under this sort of stress, they resort to cunning in order to fool their rulers and turn to deviousness in hopes of escape. Then even strict laws and harsh penalties cannot prevent villainy, because they haven't enough power. Therefore, a proverb says, "When birds are at their wit's end, they peck; when beasts are at their wit's end, they gore; and when humans are at their wit's end, they resort to trickery."

—

Enlightened people are able to criticize rulers when they see a fault, because they are mindless of reprisal. They are able to defer to the wise when they see them, because they are mindless of social status. They are able to give to those in need, because they are mindless of their own poverty.

—

People in honored positions are called honorable when they are impartial and impersonal. They are therefore called honorable but are not therefore called wise. Those who hold the land are called fair when they have standard practices and no hidden schemes. They are therefore called fair but are not therefore called smart.

When there is no official brutality to alienate the common people, and no intellectual activism to cause resentment among other leaders, the manners of all classes continue unbroken, so critics cannot grasp the situation and do not see anything to observe. This is called concealment in formlessness. Without concealment in formlessness, who can master form?

—

Moralists today forbid what is desired without finding out the basic reasons for desire; they prohibit what is enjoyed without finding out the basic reasons for enjoyment. This is like trying to dam a river with your hands.

Moralists cannot get people not to want, but they can forbid what people want; they cannot get people not to indulge, but they can prohibit what people indulge in. Even if fear of punishment makes people afraid to steal, how could that compare to freeing people from the desire to steal?

—

The government of complete people covers brilliance, obliterates ostentation, substitutes reality for intellectual knowledge, emerges from impartiality shared with all people, gets rid of seductive longings, eliminates habitual desire, and reduces anxious thoughts.

—

The reasons people commit crimes that will land them in jail, or get into trouble that will result in execution, stem from insatiability and lack of means.

—

Everyone knows that evildoers have no escape and criminals cannot get away; yet the unintelligent cannot overcome their desires and thus commit crimes leading to their own destruction.

—

The world can only be entrusted to those who are able to avoid harming their countries by global ambitions and who are able to avoid ruining themselves by national ambitions.

—

Those who know the source of law and order change to adapt to the times. Those who do not know the source of law and order change with customs. Manners and duties change with customs. Scholars make it their business to follow precedent, preserving the old based on convention, thinking that government is otherwise impossible. This is like trying to put a square peg in a round hole.

—

The reason why leaders are set up is to eliminate violence and quell disorder. Now they take advantage of the power of the people to become plunderers themselves. They are like winged tigers—why shouldn't they be eliminated? If you want to raise fish in a pond, you have to get rid of otters; if you want to raise domestic animals, you have to get rid of wolves—how much the more so when governing people!

—

Lower-level leaders ambitious for middle-level authority will lose their lower-level leadership. Middle-level leaders ambitious for upper-level authority will lose their middle-level leadership.

—

To indulge the perversities of an individual, thereby increasing troubles throughout the land, is unacceptable to natural reason.

—

If rulers are too inclined to benevolence, then the unworthy are rewarded and criminals go free. If the rulers are too inclined to punishment, then the worthy are rejected and the ignorant slaughtered. As for those who have no inclinations, they give without reward and punish without resentment.

—

When water is polluted, fish choke; when government is harsh, people rebel.

—

When society is orderly, you protect yourself with justice; when society is confused, you protect justice by yourself.

—

Duplicity cannot win a single person; wholeheartedness can win a hundred people.

—

Sages encourage good by means of what the people like, and they prohibit evil by means of what the people dislike. They reward one person, and the whole world lauds them; they punish one person, and the whole world is in awe of them. Therefore, the best reward is not expensive, and the best punishment is not excessive.

—

Sages use culture to communicate with society and use reality to do what is appropriate. They are not bound to one track; they do not stagnate or neglect to adapt. This is why their failures are few and their successes are many, why their directives are carried out and no one can deny them.

—

When sages are in high positions, the people are pleased with their government; when sages are in low positions, the people look up to their ideas. When petty people are in high positions, it is not possible to rest easy even for a moment.

—

If the rulers look upon the ruled as upon their own children, then the ruled will look upon the rulers as upon their own parents. If the rulers look upon the ruled as upon their own younger siblings, then the ruled will look upon the rulers as upon their own older siblings. When rulers look upon the ruled as upon their own children, then they will rule the world. When the ruled look upon the rulers as upon their own parents, then they will rectify the world. When rulers look upon the ruled as upon their own younger siblings, they do not find it hard to die for them. When the ruled look upon the rulers as upon their older siblings, they do not find it hard to die for them. So you cannot fight against an army of parents, children, and siblings, because of how much they have already done for one another.

—

Rulers seek two things from their subjects: they want the people to work for the country, and they want people to die for the country. The people hope for three things from their rulers: that the hungry can be fed, the weary can be given rest, and the worthy can be rewarded. If the people have fulfilled the two demands made of them by the government, but the government neglects the three things expected by the people, then even if a country is large and its people many, the militia will still be weak.

—

The martial lord of Wei asked one of his ministers what made a nation perish. The minister replied, "Numerous victories in numerous wars."

The lord said, "A nation is fortunate to win numerous victories in numerous wars—why would it perish thereby?"

The minister said, "When there are repeated wars, the people are weakened; when they score repeated victories, rulers become haughty. Let haughty rulers command weakened people, and rare is the nation that will not perish as a result."

—

An ancient scholar carrying a load of books met a recluse on the road. The recluse said, "Public servants act in response to changes, and changes occur in time; so those who know the times do not act in a fixed way. Books are produced by words, and words come from those who know; so those who know do not store books."

—

When the state of Jin marched on the state of Chu, the grandees of Chu asked the king to attack, but the king said, "Jin did not attack us during the reign of our former king; now that Jin is attacking us in my reign, this must be my fault. What can be done for this disgrace?"

The grandees said, "Jin did not attack us in the time of previous ministers; now that Jin is attacking us during our administration, it must be our fault."

The king of Chu bowed his head and wept. Then he rose and bowed to his ministers.

When the people of Jin heard of this, they said, "The king and his ministers are competing to take the blame on themselves; and how easily the king humbles himself to his subordinates! They cannot be attacked."

So that night the Jin army turned around to go home.

This is why Lao-tzu said, "Who can accept the disgrace of the nation is called the ruler of the land."

—

Once someone asked a wise man which of six leading generals would be the first to perish. The wise man named one of them, and the inquirer asked why he chose that one. The wise man said, "In his administration, harshness is taken for alertness, pleasure is taken for enlightenment, and cruelty to subordinates is taken for loyalty."

This is why Lao-tzu said, "When the government is unobtrusive, people are pure; when the government is prying, people are wanting."

—

Whatever is inappropriate in the policies of former regimes is
to be abandoned, while whatever is good in the affairs of later
days is to be adopted. There has never been any fixed constant
in manners and culture, so sages formulate manners and culture
without being ruled by manners and culture.

—

To recite the books of ancient kings is not as good as hearing
their words. Hearing their words is not as good as attaining that
whereby those words were spoken. To attain that whereby those
words were spoken is something that words cannot say. Therefore, "a way that can be spoken is not the eternal Way."

—

When a country changes its leaders repeatedly and people use
that status to do what they want and use that power to feed their
desires, yet they want to adapt to the times and deal with changes
in a uniform manner and by fixed laws, clearly they cannot manage
the responsibility.

So what sages follow is called the Way, and what they do is
called their work. The Way is like metal and stone, unchanging;
their work is like a musical instrument, which must be tuned each
time.

—

Laws and conventions are tools of government, but they are not
what constitutes government.

—

Humanity and justice are the warp and woof of society; this never
changes. If people can assess their abilities and take the time to

examine what they do, then even if changes take place daily, that is all right.

—

In ancient times people were pure, crafts were sturdy, commerce was simple, and women were chaste. Therefore, government and education were easily effective, manners and customs were easily changed. Now that society's virtues are declining and mores grow weaker, to want to govern a decadent populace with simple laws is like trying to ride a wild horse without a bit and bridle.

—

King Wen was intelligent yet still sought to learn; therefore he became wise. King Wu was brave yet still sought to learn; therefore he was victorious. Anyone who rides on the knowledge of the many becomes wise; anyone who utilizes the strength of the many prevails.

—

When a group of people unifies, a hundred people have surplus strength. Therefore, to rely on the power of one individual is sure to result in insecurity.

—

When there is no discrimination but each individual finds a suitable way of life, then the world is equalized, no one dominates another. Sages find work for all of them, so no abilities are wasted.

—

Many people are blinded by name and reputation. Few people see the reality.

—

The nature of ordinary men is to be wild when young, violent when mature, and greedy when old. Even one person undergoes a number of changes, so it is no wonder that leaders repeatedly change laws and countries repeatedly change leaders. If people use their positions to enforce their own likes and dislikes, then those in subordinate positions of responsibility will fear being unable to manage successfully.

—

In the creation of manners, it is enough just to assist realities and clarify intentions. In the creation of music, it is enough just to harmonize enjoyment and express ideas.

In a disorderly nation, words and actions are mutually contradictory; feelings and expressions are opposite. Manners are elaborated to the point of being toilsome; music is elaborated to the point of being licentious.

—

Governing a country is like weeding a garden; just get rid of the sprouts of harmful plants—that's all.

—

Fashions, manners, and customs are not people's natures but what they take in from without. Human nature is innocent; when steeped in customs for a long time, it changes. When people's natures change, they forget the origin and conform to a seeming nature.

—

Those who have attained the Way change outwardly but not inwardly. Their outward changes are their means of entering human society; their inner unchanging is their means of keeping whole. Therefore, they have a stable inner life while they can outwardly adapt to changes in others.

—

Those who do not dare to touch fire even though they have never been burned see the possibility of being burned; those who do not dare to grab a sword even though they have never been wounded see the possibility of being wounded. Viewed in this light, the perceptive can understand what has not yet occurred, and by observing a small section it is possible to know the whole body.

—

The confusion of ignorant rulers by treacherous ministers and the suspicions of petty people toward the cultivated can be seen while still subtle and clearly recognized only by sages.

—

Those who governed the world in antiquity must have understood the true conditions of human nature and destiny; their actions were not necessarily the same, but they were one in their accord with the Tao.

—

In ancient times, vehicles were not painted or engraved. Artisans did not have two crafts; scholars did not hold different offices simultaneously. Everyone kept their own jobs and did not interfere with each other. People found what suited them; things were at ease.

—

Asking for fire is not as good as getting means of making fire; depending on someone to draw water is not as good as digging a well yourself.

—

The spirit crosses mountains, and they cannot trouble it; it enters the oceans and rivers, and they cannot wet it. It is not suffocated in a narrow place, and though it spreads throughout heaven and earth, it is not filled up.

Those who do not understand this may have material resources and an artistic culture with splendid intellectual and literary activity, but none of that will help them govern the world without this understanding.

—

Those who do not see great meaning do not know that life is not worth greed. Those who have not heard great words do not know that dominion over the world is not worth considering an advantage.

—

Duty means doing what is appropriate, in accord with reason. Courtesy means controlled elegance embodying feelings.

—

When vitality and spirit are strained, they disintegrate; when ear and eye are unruly, they become exhausted. Therefore, leaders imbued with the Way stop imagining and get rid of willfulness, remaining poised in a state of clarity and openness.

—

Those who gain the benefit of power have very little in the way of holdings and very much in the way of responsibility. What they maintain is very restricted, what they control is very broad.

—

Lofty terraces and multistoried pavilions are splendid indeed, but an enlightened leader cannot enjoy them if people are homeless. Fine wine and tender meat are delicious indeed, but an enlightened leader cannot enjoy them if people are undernourished.

—

Unprincipled rulers take from the people without measuring the people's strength; they make demands on their subjects without assessing how much their subjects have. Men and women cannot attend to plowing and weaving because they have to supply the demands of the rulers; so their energies are strained and their goods are exhausted. Thus rulers and subjects hate each other.

—

In the overall scheme of nature, three years of cultivation result in one year's food surplus. Nine years produce three years' surplus, eighteen years produce six years' surplus, and twenty-seven years produce nine years' surplus. Thus even if there is a flood or a drought, the people are not reduced to desperate straits.

So if a country does not have enough surplus to last nine years, it is said to be lacking. If it does not have supplies for six years, it is said to be suffering from stress. If it does not have stores for three years, it is said to be poor. Therefore, human rulers and enlightened rulers limit what they take from their subjects and are moderate in their living.

—

Greedy leaders and harsh rulers oppress their subjects and bleed their people to satisfy their own interminable desires. Thus the commoners have no way to benefit from the harmony of heaven or walk upon the blessings of earth.

—

Food is the basis of the people; the people are the basis of the country; the country is the basis of the ruler.

—

The law of ancient kings forbade hunters to deplete the herds or take the yearlings and forbade fishers to empty the ponds. Traps and nets were not to be set before certain times; wood was not to be cut before the leaves fell; fields were not to be burned before the insects went into hibernation. Pregnant or nursing animals were not to be killed; eggs were not to be taken from nests; fish less than a foot long were not to be caught.

—

What enables a nation to survive is benevolence and justice; what enables people to live is practical virtue. A nation without justice will perish even if it is large; people without goodwill will be wounded even if they are brave.

—

The ruler is the mind of the nation. When the mind is orderly, all nodes are calm; when the mind is disturbed, all nodes are deranged. So in one whose mind is orderly, the limbs of the body forget about each other; when a country is orderly, the ruler and ministers forget about each other.

—

Humanitarianism is the manifest demonstration of accumulated benevolence; social duty is sharing human feelings and according with what is appropriate for the community.

—

Ancient leaders considered the world light and myriad things small; they equalized death and life and assimilated to change and evolution. They embraced the mind of great sages to mirror the feelings of all beings. Above, they were companions of spiritual luminosities; below, they were members of creation. If those who want to learn their Way now do not attain their clear illumination and profound sagacity, but just keep their laws and policies, clearly they cannot govern.

So to obtain ten sharp swords is not as good as mastering the art of the swordsmith.

—

The greatest simplicity is formless; the most far-reaching Way is measureless. Therefore, the sky is round without being set to a compass; the earth is straight without being set to a ruler.

—

The laws of the Three August Ones and Five Emperors of high antiquity were different in what they prescribed but equal in that they won the hearts of the people.

—

Those who value life do not destroy themselves for material gain. Those who are firm in ethics do not try to spare themselves when they see difficulty. Those greedy for money disregard their health when they see a profit to be made. Those who want a good name will not try to get it unjustly.

—

This is the way to govern a country: The rulers are not harsh; the officials are not bothersome; the intellectuals are not hypocritical; the artists are not decadent.

—

In an incoherent society, activists promote each other by mutual praise, while people of culture honor each other hypocritically.

—

Deceptive writers are deliberately prolix and confusing in order to appear wise; competing with sophistry, their interminable reflections are inconclusive, without benefit to social order.

—

The customs of a decadent society use cunning and deceit to dress up the useless.

—

No one has ever heard of anyone who avoided breaking the law and risking punishment when both hungry and cold.

—

When people have more than enough, they defer; when they have less than enough, they contend. When people defer, courtesy and justice are born; when they contend, violence and disorder arise.

—

Kindling is not sold in the forest and fish are not sold by a lake, because there is a superabundance. So when there is plenty, desires diminish; when wants are minimal, contention stops.

—

When society is orderly, the common people are upright and cannot be seduced by profit. When society is disorderly, the elite are villainous and cannot be stopped by the law.

—

The behavior of sage kings did not hurt the feelings of the people, so even while the kings enjoyed themselves the world was at peace.

The evil kings denied the truthful and declared them outlaws, so as the kings enjoyed themselves everything went to ruin.

When like and dislike began to have their say, order and chaos went their ways.

—

In ancient times there were people who lived in the primordial unknown, their spirit and energy not flowing out. Everything was peaceful to them, so they were happy and calm. Injurious energies diffused and did not harm them.

In those times, most people were wild. They didn't know east from west. They roamed around gathering food, then drummed their bellies and played when they'd eaten. Their relations were imbued with natural harmony, and they ate from the blessings of the earth.

Culture is a means of joining people. Feelings are inner connections with an impulse to act outwardly. Obliterate feelings by culture, and you lose feeling. Destroy culture by feelings, and you lose culture.

When culture is orderly and feelings are communicated, this is the peak of human development.

This means that it is a virtue to take an overall view.

—

At one time, there were no rewards given as inducements and no penalties used as threats. Manners, duties, and conscience were not defined; there was neither censure nor praise, neither kindness nor meanness. Yet the people were not aggressive, deceitful, violent, or cruel toward one another. They were still unselfconscious.

When society deteriorated, there were many people and few goods; they worked hard for a living that was nevertheless insufficient. At this point anger and contention arose, so kindness came to be valued.

Now that some people were kind and others were mean, favoritism and partisanship developed. People practiced deliberate deceit and cunning. Thus nature was lost, so duty came to be valued.

—

In the government of perfected people, mind and spirit are in place, body and nature are harmonized. In times of quiet it absorbs virtue; in times of action it applies reason. It follows nature as it is and focuses on inevitable evolution. It is clear and uncontrived, so the world spontaneously harmonizes itself; it is calm and desireless, so the people are naturally simple. There is no luck, yet no misfortune; there is no struggle, yet the needs of life are amply met. It embraces the whole land and enriches its posterity, but no one knows who or what has done it.

—

In latter-day government, there are heavy taxes on hunting, fishing, and commerce. Hatcheries are closed off; there is nowhere to string nets, nowhere to plow. The people's strength is used up by corvée labor; their wealth is exhausted by poll tax. People at home have no food; travelers have no supplies. The living have no support; the dead have no funerals. Men sell their wives and children to meet the demands placed on them by the government yet still cannot provide what is required.

—

A degenerate society is characterized by expansionism and imperialism, starting unjust military operations against innocent countries, killing innocent people, cutting off the heritage of ancient sages.

Large countries go on the offensive; small countries become defensive. People's livestock are driven off; people's children are taken captive; people's shrines are destroyed; people's prized possessions are taken away. Blood flows for a thousand miles, and skeletons litter the fields—all to satisfy the desires of greedy rulers and governments.

This is not what armies are really for. A militia is supposed to put down violence, not cause violence.

—

True leaders of society make progress when the time is right, accomplishing it justly, so they are not especially happy about it.

When the time is not right, they withdraw, deferring justly, so they are not unhappy about it.

This is why an ancient baron, who abdicated to his younger brother and is traditionally named as a paragon of virtue, starved to death in the mountains without regret. He gave up what he despised and got what he valued.

—

The art of human leadership is to manage affairs without contrivance and instruct without speaking; to be pure and calm, unmoving, unshakably consistent, delegating matters to subordinates according to custom, so that duties are accomplished without strain.

—

When the territory is large because of virtue and the leadership is honored because of virtue, that is best.

When the territory is large because of justice and the leadership is honored because of justice, that is next best.

When the territory is large because of strength and the leadership is honored because of strength, that is lowest.

—

A disorderly nation seems full; an orderly nation seems empty. A moribund nation seems lacking; a surviving nation seems to have an overabundance. Emptiness does not mean there are no people, but that all keep to their work; fullness does not mean there are many people, but that all seek trivialities. Having an overabundance does not mean many possessions, but that desires are moderate and affairs minimal. Lack does not mean there are no goods, but that the people are impulsive and their expenditures are many.

—

Covetous people with many desires are lulled to sleep by power and profit, seduced into longing for fame and status. They wish to rise in the world through exceptional cunning, so their vitality and spirit are depleted daily and become further and further away.

—

Those desirous of fortune may create disaster, while those desirous of gain may cleave to what is harmful. Therefore, those who are at peace without contrivance will be imperiled if they lose that whereby they are at peace. And those who govern without striving will fall into chaos if they lose that whereby they govern.

—

A good rider doesn't forget the horse; a good archer doesn't forget the bow; a good leader doesn't forget the populace.

If leaders can truly love and truly benefit the populace, then everyone can follow. But even a child rebels against an unloving and abusive parent.

There is something of paramount importance in the world, but it is not power or status. There is great wealth, but it is not gold or jewels. There is a full life, but it is not measured in length of years.

When you look into the source of the mind and return to its essential nature, that is what is important. When you are content with your feelings, you are wealthy. When you understand the division between death and life, then your life is full.

—

The eyes and ears of enlightened leaders are not strained; their vitality and spirit are not exhausted. When things come up, they observe their changes, and when events happen, they respond to their developments. When there is no confusion near at hand, there is order far away.

—

Rulers of disorderly nations strive to expand their territory; they do not strive for humanity and justice. They strive to elevate their status; they do not strive for the virtue of the Way. This is abandoning the means of survival and creating the causes of destruction. For this reason ancient despots who were deposed and imprisoned did not repudiate their actions or review their errors; they just regretted not having killed their successors when they had the chance.

—

The world can be gained but not taken; rulership can be accepted but not sought. Rely on intelligence, and people will contest it; rely on power, and people will fight it.

It is not possible to render people completely ignorant, but it is possible to render them unable to use their intelligence against you. It is not possible to render people completely powerless, but it is possible to render them unable to use their power against you. These two things are always in the long view.

—

The crafty are good at calculating; the knowing are good at fore-seeing.

—

The Tao is mysterious and silent, with no appearance, no model. Its size is infinite, its depth immeasurable. Yet it participates in human development, though ordinary knowledge cannot grasp it.

In antiquity, when Shennong, "The Agricultural Genius," governed the land, his spirit did not race within his chest; his wisdom was not used for expansionism. He had a kind and sincere heart.

There were timely showers of sweet rain, and the five grains flourished. There was growth in spring, maturation in summer, harvest in autumn, storage in winter.

There were monthly reviews and timely considerations. At the end of the year the fruits of labor were presented, and the crops of each grain were tasted in season.

In the impartial care of the enlightened leader, the Agricultural Genius, the people were simple, straightforward, and honest. They obtained sufficient goods without contending; they accomplished their work without straining their bodies. They relied on the sustenance of heaven and earth and harmonized with them.

Therefore, authority was strict but not tested; punishments were established but not used; laws were simple and not elaborate.

Thus it was that the reign of Shennong was one of genius.

—

Those who comprehend the Tao are not focused only on themselves; they are also connected to the world.

—

If you want to know the way of the sky, observe the seasonal cycles. If you want to know the way of the earth, find out what kind of trees grow there. If you want to know the way of people, let them have what they want.

—

If you stretch out a net where birds will fly by, it is only one eye of the net that catches a bird, but if you make a net of one eye, you'll never catch a bird.

—

When you go to market in the morning you run, but when you go by the market in the evening you walk, because your need is not there any more.

—

In ancient times, when the state of Chu was going to attack the state of Song, the philosopher Mozi heard of this and lamented. He set off from his native state of Lu and walked for ten days and nights. His feet were blistered and calloused, but he didn't rest until he got to Chu, tearing off pieces of his clothing to wrap his feet as he went along.

When he saw the king of Chu, Mozi said, "I heard you are raising an army to attack Song. Are you attacking Song with an infallible plan already worked out to take it? Have you forgotten about the suffering and hardship you will cause the people? If your army were going to be halted and your weapons broken down, and you were to be infamous for injustice without having gained a square foot of territory, would you still attack Song?"

The king said, "If I were certain to fail to take Song, and would also be doing an injustice, why would I attack it?"

Mozi said, "The way I see it, you will surely do violence to justice and also fail to conquer Song."

The king said, "I have the most skilled craftsman in the world to construct siege towers. If I set them up to attack Song, how can I fail to take it?"

Mozi then told the king to have his artisan set up a siege, saying that he would show how a defense could be made. The master craftsman set up nine sieges, and Mozi foiled every one, not letting any through.

Now the king of Chu put down his arms and gave up on attacking Song.

Another time, there was a man named Duan Ganmu who gave up his career and stayed at home. The lord of Wei went to his town and formally paid his respects to the townspeople. When his servant asked him why he was doing this, the lord replied, "Because Duan Ganmu lives here."

The servant said, "Duan Ganmu is a man of no account. Isn't it going too far to pay respects to his town like this?"

The lord said, "Duan Ganmu does not chase after power and profit but takes the way of the enlightened to heart. Though he lives anonymously in a poor neighborhood, his good name is known far and wide. How can I not honor his town?"

The lord went on, "He is radiant with virtue; I am radiant with power. He is ethically rich; I am materially rich. Power is not as honorable as virtue; possessions are not as noble as ethics. Even if he could change places with me, he wouldn't do it."

Later, when the kingdom of Qin had raised an army to attack Wei, one of the peers of Qin opposed the plan, saying, "Duan Ganmu is a wise man, and his ruler honors him. Everyone knows this; all the lords have heard of it. If we raise an army to attack Wei, would this not be unethical?"

Because of this, the king of Qin gave up his plan to attack Wei.

Mozi ran a thousand miles to secure the survival of Chu and Song; Duan Ganmu pacified Qin and Wei without leaving home. Action and inaction are opposite, but they can both be used to preserve nations. This is what is called reaching the same goal by different roads.

—

People's knowledge of things is shallow, yet they want that knowledge to light up everywhere in the land, keeping everything in mind. If they do not depend upon the mathematics of principle, and use only their own subjective ability, it will not be long before they reach a final impasse. Conventional knowledge is not sufficient to govern the land.

An evil king of old had phenomenal strength; he killed giant tortoises in the sea and captured bears on land. The man who overthrew him had but a small force, yet he stopped the evil king and took him captive. As this shows, virility alone is not sufficient to govern the land.

Since conventional knowledge is insufficient to govern and virility is not enough to be strong, then human talent is not necessarily to be trusted as enlightened.

A ruler who does not descend from the upper part of the temple yet knows beyond the four seas is one who recognizes things by means of things and knows people by means of people.

There is no limit to what accumulated power can lift. Whatever is done by the knowledge of many succeeds.

—

If you ride on the knowledge of the multitude, it is easy to gain dominion; if you only use your own mind, you cannot even preserve yourself.

—

When there is overt public acceptance of what is still only an idea in the mind of the leadership, it means truthfulness has hit its mark.

—

When people are skillfully employed, they are like the legs of a millipede—numerous without interfering with each other. They are like lips and teeth—hard and soft rubbing together without hurting each other.

—

When manners and habits are changed without any commands or directives being issued, that can only be by the influence of kindness—laws and punishments are insufficient to bring it about.

—

The abilities of one man are insufficient to govern a single household; but follow the measures of true reason, based on the nature of the universe, and the whole world is equal.

—

Leaders see with the eyes of the whole nation, hear with the ears of the whole nation, think with the knowledge of the whole nation, and move with the strength of the whole nation.

For this reason, their directives reach all the way to the lower echelons, while the feelings of the masses come to the notice of the leaders.

—

Those who reign by attainment of the Way may have no skills themselves, but they can indeed employ the skilled. If you do not attain the Way, even if you have many skills they are useless.

—

In ancient times, when sage kings ruled, their government and education were egalitarian, and their charity extended to all. Those above and those below were of like mind; superiors and subordinates associated cordially. There was enough food and clothing, enough housing and employment. Fathers were kind; children were filial; elder siblings were good; younger siblings were obedient. The living bore no grudges, and the dying had no resentment. The world was harmonious, and people attained their wishes.

—

No one has ever heard of a country being chaotic when individuals are orderly, and no one has heard of a country being orderly when individuals are unruly. If a rule is not straight, it cannot be used to make a square; if a compass is not correct, it cannot be used to make a circle. The individual is the rule and compass of affairs: no one has ever heard of being able to rectify others while being crooked oneself.

—

Haughty and overbearing rulers do not have loyal ministers; clever talkers are not necessarily trusted.

—

The way of the ruler is round, revolving endlessly, with a nurturing spiritual influence, open and selfless, harmonious, always in the background and never in the forefront.

The way of the minister is square, deliberating on what is right and applying appropriate measures, initiating suggestions for action, keeping to the job with distinct clarity, thus achieving success.

Therefore, when ruler and minister differ in their ways, there is order; when they make their ways identical, there is disorder. When they each manage to do what is appropriate for them and handle their own responsibilities, then superior and subordinate have the means to work together.

—

There are physical and mental limits to what a person can do. This is why someone with one body occupies one position, and someone with one skill works at one craft.

When their strength is up to a task, people do not consider it a heavy burden. When their ability suits a craft, people do not consider it hard to do.

—

People may go to a certain place by boat or by carriage; though they take different routes in either case, their destination is one. People with fine figures do not all have the same bodies; beauties do not all have the same faces; but all of them are pleasing to the eye. Pears, oranges, dates, and chestnuts do not taste the same, but all of them are palatable. There are people who get rich by stealing, but a rich person is not necessarily a thief. There are people who are poor because of their integrity, but a poor person does not necessarily have integrity.

—

There are ways to evaluate people. If they are in positions of high status, observe what they promote. If they are wealthy, observe what they give. If they are poor, observe what they refuse to accept. If they are of low status, observe what they refuse to do. If they are covetous, observe what they will not take. See them change difficulties, and you can know their courage. Move them with joy and happiness, and you can observe their self-control. Entrust them with goods and money, and you can assess their humanity. Shake them with fear, and you can know their discipline.

—

Rulers have to be careful about whom they appoint to office. If the right people are entrusted with responsibilities, then the nation is orderly; superiors and subordinates harmonize; the officials are kind, and the common people are loyal. If the wrong people are entrusted with responsibilities, then the nation is imperiled; superiors and subordinates oppose each other; the officials are resentful, and the common people are disorderly. Therefore, a single inappropriate appointment means a lifetime of trouble.

—

If the ruler is truly upright, then honest people are entrusted with affairs, and the treacherous go into hiding. If the ruler is not upright, then evil people achieve their aims, and the trustworthy go into concealment.

—

Let rulers hold to uprightness and fairness as a plumb line, and officials who come to them with dishonest designs might as well be breaking eggs by throwing them at a rock or trying to set fire to water.

There was a king who liked slender waists, and people starved themselves to become thin. Another king admired bravery, and people endangered themselves and fought duels to the death. As we can see from these examples, the handle of authority and power easily influences fashions and changes morals.

—

When the directives of the leadership are ignored because of factionalism, laws are broken out of treachery, intellectuals busy themselves fabricating clever deceits, mettlesome men occupy themselves fighting, administrators monopolize authority, petty bureaucrats hold power, and cliques curry favor to manipulate the leadership. Then, even though the nation may seem to exist, the ancients would say it has perished.

—

When subjects do not get what they want from their rulers, the rulers cannot get what they seek from their subjects either. What rulers and subjects give each other is motivated by reciprocity, for which subjects will exert themselves to the full and lay down their lives in the interests of their rulers, while rulers will grant honors for the benefit of their subjects.

If rulers cannot reward unworthy subjects, then subjects cannot die for unworthy rulers. If the blessings bestowed by rulers do not reach the citizens, and yet the rulers want to use the people, this is like whipping a bucking bronco. This is similar to expecting crops to ripen without rain—an impossibility.

—

If rich rewards are given to those without merit, and high titles are given to those who have not worked, then people in office will be lazy about their duties, and idlers will advance rapidly.

If people are put to death without having committed any crime, and honest people are punished, then those who cultivate themselves will not be encouraged to do good, and evildoers will think little of treason.

In an enlightened government, the state executes criminals without any anger on the part of the ruler. The court rewards the worthy without any involvement on the part of the ruler. Those who are executed do not resent the ruler because the punishment fits the crime. Those who are rewarded do not attribute it to the ruler because it was brought about by their accomplishments. Thus the people know that it is up to them whether they are punished or rewarded.

—

Without serenity, there is no way to illuminate one's character. Without calm, there is no way to persevere. Without magnanimity, there is no way to embrace everyone. Without kindness, there is no way to care for all the people. Without fairness, there is no way to make sound judgments.

Therefore, a wise ruler employs people the way a skilled craftsman works wood. Large and small, long and short—there is an appropriate use for everything. Ruler and compass, square and round—each has its application. Though shapes be different and materials diverse, there are none that cannot be used.

Even the most virulent poison can be useful in the hands of a skilled physician. Since even the materials of the forest and field are not wasted, why should people be rejected?

Now, when people are not elected to court or honored in the provinces, that does not mean they are unworthy but only that the positions available to them are not their proper work.

—

Someone with great overall strategy should not be pressed for a quick fix. Someone with small knowledge should not be entrusted with a great work.

People have their specific talents; things have their specific forms. Some find the responsibility for one too heavy, while others find the responsibility for a hundred still light.

Therefore, petty-minded policies will inevitably cause loss of the overall integrity of society. Those who do not miss an election on small matters may lose a really important choice.

A badger cannot be used to catch oxen; a tiger cannot be used to do the mousing. Now, the talents of people today may be such that they want to pacify the whole land and win the allegiance of other countries, preserve endangered nations and perpetuate dying peoples. Their aspiration is to make the way straight, correct what has gone awry, settle embroilments, and bring order to confusion. If personal courtesy is demanded of them, then cunning and crafty people will get ahead by flattery and ingratiation while going along with provincial vulgarities to get the attention of the people.

If people are entrusted with political authority in this way, that is like using an axe to shave hair or using a knife to fell a tree—both are out of place.

—

Useful suggestions should not be rejected just because they come from people in low positions, nor should useless suggestions be followed just because they come from people in high positions. Right and wrong are not a question of social status. Enlightened leaders listen to their ministers: if their plans are useful, the leaders do not look down on them because of rank; and if what they say is feasible, the leaders do not care about how they say it.

Ignorant rulers are not like this. As far as their familiars and associates are concerned, even if they are dishonest, the rulers cannot see it; and when it comes to strangers and people of lowly status, even when they are diligent and loyal, the leaders cannot know it. Those who have something to say are badgered about their choice of words, while those who have criticisms are punished as if they had committed a crime. If you want to illumine the land and sustain the communities this way, that is like covering your ears to listen to music or covering your eyes to look at a painting—even if you have good hearing and eyesight, you will still be far off.

—

If people can use what is not beneficial to them in such a way as to benefit others, that is acceptable. When a madman runs off and someone runs after him, both are running in the same direction, but they're running for different purposes. When a man is drowning in the water and someone goes in to save him, both are in the water, but they've gone in for different reasons.

—

Using the measures and regulations of one generation or one age to govern the world is like the case of a traveler in a boat who drops his sword in the middle of the river and notches the edge of the boat to mark the spot where the sword fell; then he goes back to the riverbank that evening to look for the sword below the notch on the boat. He is far from knowing what is what.

—

If you follow limited examples and do not know how to travel through heaven and earth, you could not be more confused.

—

If the rope is short, it cannot be used to draw water from a deep well; if the vessel is small, it cannot be used to hold what is large—they simply cannot handle the job.

—

Law derives from justice; justice derives from what suits the community. What suits the community accords with the hearts of the people. This is the essence of government.

So those who comprehend the basis are not confused by ramifications, and those who see what is essential are not confused by details.

Law does not come down from the heavens, nor does it spring up from the earth. It develops among people and winds up in self-correction.

Therefore, those who have it in themselves do not deny it in others; those who lack it in themselves do not seek it from others. What is set up for the lower echelons is not to be neglected in the higher echelons, and what is forbidden to the people is not to be done by the ruler.

A lost nation is not one that lacks a ruler but one that lacks law. Distortion of law does not mean there is no law; it means there is law but it is not applied. Thus, it is as if there is no law.

Therefore, when leaders establish law, they personally act as models and exemplars. This is why their directives are carried out throughout the land.

Confucius said, "When people are personally upright, others go along with them even though they are not commanded to do so; when people are not upright themselves, others will not follow them even if ordered to do so." So when leaders themselves are subject to regulations, then their directives are carried out by the people.

—

In an ideal state, those of high social standing are not given lighter sentences, and those of low social status are not given heavier sentences. Those who break the law are punished even if they are otherwise good, while those who conform to the law are not punished even if they are worthless. This is how the public Way is kept open while the private way is stopped.

—

In antiquity, overseers of works were appointed to see that the people were not negligent; leaders were set up to see to it that overseers of works did not act arbitrarily. Law used social order, duty and justice, to prevent the ruler from making arbitrary decisions.

When people cannot indulge their personal whims, then the Way prevails. When the Way prevails, then order is attained. Thus there is a return to noncontrivance.

Noncontrivance does not mean stagnant inaction. It is an expression used to mean that nothing comes from the ego.

—

Those who govern do not value self-righteousness; they value the impossibility of doing wrong. Therefore, it is said, "Rather than forbid ambition, let there be nothing to desire; rather than forbid contention, let there be nothing to usurp." In this way people's talents are discerned, and fairness is put into practice. Those with more than enough stop at good measure, while those with less than enough find employment. Thus the land can be unified.

—

When delight and anger form in the heart, and desires are outwardly visible, then those in office depart from rectitude and curry favor with their superiors, and administrators bend the law and go along with trends. Rewards are not appropriate to achievements; punishments do not correspond to crimes. Superiors and subordinates become alienated; rulers and ministers resent each other. Thus, when those in charge of political affairs curry favor with the rulers, they are not blamed for mistakes or punished for crimes. Then there is disorder in government, which wisdom cannot resolve; slander and praise sprout up, which intelligence cannot clarify. Unless there is a rectification of basics and a return to naturalness, leaders will come under increasing strain while administrators become increasingly negligent.

—

Those who use their skills to struggle for power start out in the sun and end up in the shade. Those who use their wits to govern countries start out with order and end up with chaos.

Let water flow downward, and no one can stop it; but when it comes to driving it upward, only an engineer can do it. Therefore, when embellishment is dominant, substance is covered; when the devious are clever, the upright are impeded.

Virtue can be used to cultivate oneself; it cannot be used to make others violent. The Way can be used to govern oneself; it cannot be used to make others unruly. Even if one has the capacity of sages, in an inopportune age of violence and chaos one can thereby preserve oneself intact, but one cannot thereby command rulership.

—

The way of leadership is not for doing but for not doing. What does nondoing mean? It means that the intelligent do not act on rank, the benevolent do not give based on rank, and the brave are not violent because of rank. These can be called nondoing.

—

When leadership is established to unify the people, if the leadership is consistent, there is order, and if the leadership is inconsistent, there is disorder.

—

Find the source of destiny, master the mentality, bring to reason liking and disliking, adjust feelings and temperament appropriately, and the Way of government is attained.

When you find the source of destiny, you are not confused by calamity or fortune. When you master your mentality, you are not joyful or angry at random. When you bring reason to liking and disliking, you do not crave what is useless. When you adjust your feelings and temperament appropriately, your desires are not excessive.

When you are not confused by calamity or fortune, your action and repose follow reason. When you are not joyful or angry at random, rewards and penalties are not distorted. When you do not crave what is useless, you do not injure your nature by desire. When your desires are not excessive, you develop your nature and know contentment.

These four things are not found externally and are not gotten from others. They are attained within oneself.

—

When benevolence is overextended, it becomes weakness; and if you are weak, you lack dignity. When sternness is overextended, it becomes ferocity; and if you are fierce, you lack gentility. When liking is overextended, it becomes indulgence; and if you are indulgent, you lack authority. When punishment is overextended, it becomes cruelty; and if you are cruel, you have no friends.

—

Seeing the yielding and soft being invaded, those who do not know the Way strive to be hard and strong; seeing the hard and strong perish, they strive to be yielding and soft. Such are those who lack the basis to rule within, while their seeing and hearing run outward in confusion. Therefore, they have no stable course all their lives.

—

Right and wrong are situational. In the appropriate situation, nothing is wrong. Without the appropriate situation, nothing is right.

—

What is right in one case is not what is right in another; what is wrong in one case is not what is wrong in another.

—

Nowadays moralists extol the culture of antiquity but do not put it into practice; thus they speak of what they do not do. They criticize the present age but do not reform it; thus they do what they criticize. Therefore, they may use all of their power and reflection, but it is of no benefit to social order; they may exhaust their spirits and knowledge, but it is of no help to the time. Contemporary artists like to depict ghosts and sprites but not dogs and horses. Why? Because ghosts and sprites do not appear in every age, while dogs and horses can be seen every day.

—

To survive peril and quell disorder cannot be done without wisdom. Were it a matter of following precedents, even fools have more than enough. Therefore, enlightened leaders do not enforce useless laws or listen to ineffectual words.

—

Birth and maturation must have the vital energy of harmony. That is why the Way of sages is broad yet exacting, strict yet warm, gentle but direct, powerful but human. What is too hard snaps, and what is too soft folds; sages are between hardness and softness, thus finding the root of the Way.

—

There are three dangers in the world: To have many privileges but few virtues is the first danger. To be high in rank but low on ability is the second danger. To receive a large salary without personally accomplishing much is the third danger. So, "people may gain by loss and may lose by gain."

—

Something desired for its advantages may turn out to be harmful, while something intended to hurt others may on the contrary help them. It is imperative to examine the reversal of benefit and injury, the door of calamity and fortune.

—

Praise may cause people trouble; criticism may help them.

—

Everyone strives to be prepared to solve problems, but no one actually knows how to cause problems not to arise. It is easier to cause problems not to arise than it is to solve problems, yet no one actually knows how to work on this; so you cannot talk to anyone about such arts.

—

Those who have the Way can respond to the unexpected without lack and can escape from trouble when they meet it.

—

Mariners who are lost and cannot tell which direction they are headed have only to look at the North Star to find out. Essential nature is the North Star of human beings. If they have the means of seeing themselves, they will not miss the feelings of others. If they have no means of seeing themselves, they will be agitated and strive in confusion.

If you indulge desires so much as to lose your essential nature, nothing you do is ever right: to train yourself in this way leads to danger; to govern a nation in this way leads to chaos; to take up arms in this way leads to defeat. So those who do not hear of the Way have no means of nurturing the essential nature.

—

When those who enter a country follow its customs, and when those who go into a home observe its decorum, they can enter without breaking rules, go in without offense.

—

Etiquette is an embellishment of substantiality; humanity is an effect of grace. Therefore, etiquette depends on human feelings and tailors embellishments for them, while humanity shows up and becomes evident in the way people look. When etiquette does not exceed substantiality, and humanity does not mean giving too much, that is the way of an orderly society.

—

To act in accord with nature is called the Way; to attain the celestial nature is called virtue. When nature has been lost, humanitarianism is valued; when the Way has been lost, duty is valued. Therefore, when humanitarianism and duty are established, the Way and its virtue have shifted; when ritual and music adorn it, pure simplicity is lost. When right and wrong are formulated, the peasants are blinded; when pearls and jades are prized, everyone competes.

—

When water accumulates, it breeds predatory fish. When earth accumulates, it breeds cannibalistic beasts. When rites and duties become decorations, they breed artificial and hypocritical people.

—

People are comfortable in large houses, but birds are distressed when they get into them. Deep mountain forests are delightful to tigers and leopards, but humans are scared when they go into them. Deep ponds are suitable for turtles, but people drown in them. Classical music is enjoyed by humans, but birds are alarmed when they hear it. Cliff-hanging trees are fun for monkeys, but people would be petrified if they climbed them. Forms vary, and natures differ; so, what can be enjoyable can also be distressing, and what can be secure can also be perilous.

—

Cultivated people can live only by justice; if they lose justice, they lose their raison d'être. Infantile people can live only by desires; if they lose their desires, they have no way to live. Cultivated people fear loss of justice; infantile people fear loss of material advantages. By observing what they fear, you can tell their differences.

—

Rich are the rewards of the generous; profound are the calamities of the resentful. Never have there been any who gave little yet could expect much or any who harbored resentment yet had no troubles. So, by looking into the source of people's actions, sages can tell their consequences.

—

The way of sages is like setting up a keg of wine at a crossroads;
passersby ladle out more or less, according to their individual needs.
Therefore, the way to win one person is the way to win a hundred
people. If people deal with those below them in the same terms as
what they wish from those above them, who would not be grateful?
If people worked for those above them on the same terms as what
they want from those below them, who would not be glad?

—

An ancient sage king warned, "Be careful of each day that goes by,
with the greatest possible caution. No one stumbles over a mountain, but people do trip over anthills." So, the fact that people
generally slight small problems and subtle matters is the very
reason they have so many regrets. To worry about trouble after it
happens is like a sick man seeking good treatment only when his
condition has become critical.

—

Whenever people initiate undertakings, they invariably begin by
using their knowledge to consider and assess; only then do they
dare to define their strategy. It may turn out profitably, or it may
turn out harmfully; this is the difference between the foolish and
the wise.

Clearly it is natural to consider wisdom the key factor in the
question of survival or destruction, the door of calamity and
fortune. Countless are those who have risen up and tried to use it,
then fallen and drowned in difficulties.

If you knew how to do what is right, undertakings could be
carried out. This is a road on which all the world could arrive.

So, wisdom and reflection are the gate and door of calamity
and fortune; action and rest are the hinges of profit and loss. The

evolution of affairs and the government of nations are completed only after waiting. Those who do not drown in difficulties succeed; so it is imperative to be careful.

—

In a confused nation, those whom everyone praises are rewarded even if they have done nothing to merit it.

—

The way of rulers is to live quietly to cultivate themselves and to live frugally to lead those below. If rulers live quietly, those below will not be restless; if rulers live frugally, the citizens will not resent them.

—

In a degenerate society, those who possess the wealth of the land and are in positions of authority over others exhaust the energy of the common people to serve their own sensual desires.

—

To wish to be a partner of evolution and respond to the times by means of the transformations of a single generation is like wearing cloth in winter and leather in summer. You cannot make a hundred shots with the same aim; you cannot go through a whole year with one set of clothing. Your aim must conform to high and low; your clothing must be suited to cold and heat.

So when the generation is different, things transform; as time passes, customs change. Therefore, sages consider the society when they establish laws, and they initiate undertakings according to the times. Thus, the differences in the laws of enlightened leaders are not due to conscious attempts to contradict or reverse one another; they are due to the differences in the times and the societies. That is why they didn't take the laws already established as rules but took for their rule the very reason why laws are laws. The reason for laws to be laws is the way they change with evolving developments. The greatest value is in those who can change with evolving developments.

—

Let individuals suit their natures, be secure in their abodes, live as best they can, and exercise their capabilities. In this way even the ignorant will be found to have strong points, and even the intelligent will be found to have weaknesses.

—

Horses cannot be used to bear heavy loads; oxen cannot be used to chase the swift. Lead cannot be used to make swords; bronze cannot be used to make crossbows. Iron cannot be used to make boats; wood cannot be used to make pots. Employ them appropriately, use them where they fit, and all things and all beings are equal as one.

—

Things are not valuable or worthless; people are not high or low. When valued for what is valued in them, everything and everyone is valuable. When debased for what is base in them, everything and everyone is worthless.

A raw jade cannot be too thick; a sword edge cannot be too thin. Lacquer cannot be too black; powder cannot be too white. These are opposites, but they are equal in their requirement, whose function is one.

—

In early spring, trees are not to be felled, nests are not to be disturbed, pregnant animals are not to be killed, and birds' eggs are not to be taken.

In midspring, streams and marshes are not to be exhausted, ponds are not to be drained, and mountain forests are not to be burned. No major projects that would hinder agriculture are to be undertaken.

In late spring, repair dams, open canals, and clean the roads. Do not allow the mulberry trees to be cut. Promote home industry, and see to it that all craftsmanship is of good quality.

In early summer, do not start projects that involve moving earth, and do not cut down large trees. Encourage agriculture, and keep animals from damaging the grain. Gather and store medicinal herbs.

In midsummer, do not burn charcoal, and do not sun-bleach cloth. Let cities and towns stay open, and do not exact tariffs or taxes on goods. Remember widows and widowers, and help them get over their losses.

As the days grow longer, yin and yang struggle; death and life divide. Cultivated people regulate their diet and behavior at this time, being careful not to be overactive, being moderate in sensual enjoyments, and eating lightly.

In late summer, the fisherfolk take in huge fish and tortoises, and the foresters bring in lumber and thatch. People carry out charity drives, pay respects to the dead, visit the sick, and look in on the elderly.

At this time the trees are in their full flourishing, so they should not be cut down. Nor should massive construction projects, demonstrations, or military actions be undertaken.

In the beginning of autumn, the harvest begins. Make sure that levees are in good condition, so as to be prepared against flash floods. Fix city walls, and repair buildings and houses.

In midautumn, the time is right for urban construction projects. Dig drainage canals, and repair granaries. Store the harvest from the summer crops, and plant wheat for spring. Make measurements uniform: equalize scales, and rectify weights and measures. Regulate the customs and markets; let traveling merchants bring in their wares for the convenience of the people.

In late autumn, hunters practice with their weapons, and ceremonies propitiating animals are carried out. Brushwood is cut and made into charcoal; roads are opened, and highways are cleared.

In early winter, honor the dead, and remember orphans and widows. Look to the future to see what may lie ahead. Stock up for the winter, repair outer walls, patrol the streets, repair bolts, be careful of keys, and lock up valuable papers. Repair border fortifications and block off small paths.

In midwinter, there should be no major excavation, construction, or other undertaking requiring the mobilization of a large number of people. Thieves should be arrested at once, and dissolute con artists should be punished immediately. Patrol the streets, be careful of your houses, double your security, and attend to the women.

At this time the days reach their shortest. Cultured people regulate their consumption and behavior, staying remote and keeping quiet, abstaining from sensual stimulation, and resting the body to stabilize themselves physically and psychologically.

In late winter, the fisherfolk start fishing; the farmers prepare their seed, calculate the plowing, repair the plows and ready the hoes, and collect firewood. Farmers are to be allowed to rest and not made to work. The people acknowledge their respect for the mountains, forests, and rivers.

—

The perceptions of eye and ear are not sufficient to distinguish the inner designs of things; intellectual discourse is not sufficient to determine right and wrong. Those who use their wits to govern have a hard time maintaining a nation; only those who realize universal harmony and keep to spontaneous response can do it.

On Warfare

Those who assist human leaders with the Way
    do not coerce the world with weapons; these
    things are apt to backfire.
Brambles grow where an army has been; there are
    always bad years after a war.
Therefore the skillful are effective, that is all; they
    do not presume to grab power thereby.

                 —Lao-tzu, *Tao-te Ching*

Those who used arms in ancient times did not do so to expand their territory or obtain wealth. They did so for the survival and continuity of nations on the brink of destruction and extinction, to settle disorder in the world, and to get rid of what harmed the common people.

—

Sages' use of arms is like combing hair or thinning sprouts: a few are removed for the benefit of many. There is no harm greater than killing innocent people and supporting unjust rulers. There is no calamity worse than exhausting the world's resources to provide for the desires of an individual.

—

People have feelings about food and clothing that things cannot satisfy. Therefore, when they live together they do not share equally. If they do not get what they want, they fight. When they fight, the strong terrorize the weak, and the bold invade the timid.

—

When greedy and gluttonous people plundered the world, the people were in turmoil and could not be secure in their homes. There were sages who rose up, struck down the forceful and violent, settled the chaos of the age, leveled the unevenness, removed the pollution, clarified the turbulence, and secured the imperiled. Therefore, humankind was able to survive.

—

The military operations of effective leaders are considered philosophically, planned strategically, and supported justly. They are not intended to destroy what exists but to preserve what is perishing. Therefore, when they hear that a neighboring nation oppresses its people, they raise armies and go to the border, accusing that nation of injustice and excess.

When the armies reach the suburbs, the commanders say to their troops, "Do not cut down trees, do not disturb graveyards, do not burn crops or destroy stores, do not take common people captive, and do not steal domestic animals."

Then the announcement is made: "The ruler of such-and-such a country shows contempt for heaven and the spirits, imprisoning and executing the innocent. This is a criminal before heaven, an enemy to the people."

The coming of the armies is to oust the unjust and restore the virtuous. Those who lead plunderers of the people, in defiance of nature, die themselves, and their clans are extinguished. Those who get their families to listen to reason are enfranchised with their families; those who get their villages and towns to listen are rewarded with their villages and towns; those who get their counties to listen are enfeoffed with their counties; and those who get their states to listen are ennobled in their states.

The conquering of the nation does not extend to its people;

it removes the leadership and changes the government, honoring excellent knights, exposing the wise and good, helping the orphaned and widowed, treating the poor and destitute mercifully, freeing prisoners, and rewarding the meritorious.

The peasants await such armies with open doors, preparing food to supply them, only worried that they won't come.

So when the leadership is unguided, the people wish for military action as they wish for rain during a drought and seek to quench their thirst. Who will cross swords with a righteous army under these conditions? The supreme attainment of a just military action is to finish its mission without fighting.

As for military actions of latter-day societies, even though the rulers are unguided and lack the Way, all of them set up fortifications for defense. And when they go on the attack, it is not to stop the violent and remove the destructive; it is to invade land and enlarge their territory.

This is why things come to where there are corpses lying about with their blood streaming together before them, yet successful leadership rarely emerges. It is because it is their own contrivance; leaders are acting on their own account.

—

Those who make war to gain lands cannot fully become kings of those lands, and those who make war in their own interests cannot make their accomplishments stand.

Many people help those who initiate projects to benefit others; many people leave those who initiate projects to benefit themselves.

Those who are helped by the majority will surely be strong even if they themselves are weak, while those who are deserted by the majority will certainly perish no matter how big they are.

—

When armies lose the Way, they are weak; when they attain the Way, they are strong. When generals lose the Way, they are inept; when they attain the Way, they are skillful. When nations attain the Way, they survive; when they lose the Way, they perish.

The Way means to embody the round and emulate the square, turn away from the dark and embrace the light, be flexible culturally and firm militarily, act unobtrusively yet express enlightenment, change and transform without fixation and attain the source of unity, thereby to respond without bias. This is called spiritual illumination.

The round is sky; the square is earth. The sky is round and has no sides, so you cannot see its form. The earth is square and has no edge, so no one can look into its door. The sky nurtures creation without form; the earth develops growth without calculation. Who knows what is stored in the vastness of their totality?

—

In a military action embodying the Way, the war chariots are not launched, the horses are not saddled, the drums do not thunder, and the banners are not unfurled. Arrows are not shot, and swords do not taste blood. Courts do not change ranks, merchants do not leave the markets, and peasants do not leave the fields.

When there is an urgent call for justice, great nations will become allies and small states will follow. This is based on the will of the people, to get rid of pillagers and plunderers for them.

So those with common interests will die together; those with common feelings will develop together; those with common desires will strive together; those with common aversions will help each other. If you move in accord with the Way, the world will respond to you; think of the interests of the people, and the world will fight for you.

When hunters chase game, some ride and some go on foot, each exerting himself fully. No one threatens them with punishment, yet they help each other break through thickets, because they have the same interest.

When they are crossing a river in the same boat and it runs into a squall, the children of a hundred families will immediately help each other like right and left hands without any question of reward, because they have the same trouble.

Therefore, the military operations of enlightened leaders are to eliminate destructiveness for the world, so all the people share the advantage in common.

—

When people serve as militia in the same spirit as children doing something for their parents or older siblings, then the force of their power is like an avalanche—who can withstand it?

—

When you use arms well, you employ people to work for their own benefit. When you use arms badly, you employ people to work for your own benefit. When you employ people to work for their own benefit, anyone in the world can be employed. When you employ people to work for your own benefit, then you will find few.

—

Everyone in the world knows how to manage details, but no one knows how to work on cultivating the basis.

They leave out the root yet try to set up the branches. Now there are many things that can help their army win but few that can guarantee victory. Good armaments and equipment, abundant supplies, and many troops are of great assistance to an army, but victory is not therein.

—

The way to certain victory is to always have unfathomable wisdom and an unfailing Way.

—

The basis of military victory or defeat is in government. If government effectively rules the people and those below cleave to those above, then the militia is strong. If the people prevail over the government and those below turn against those above, then the militia is weak.

So, when virtue and justice are sufficient to embrace all the people, public works are sufficient to handle urgent needs, elections are sufficient to win the hearts of the intelligent, and thoughtful planning is sufficient to know the dispositions of strength and weakness—this is the basis of certain victory.

—

Having extensive territory and a large population is not enough to constitute strength. Having strong armor and sharp weapons is not enough to win victory. Having high walls and deep moats is not enough to ensure security. Having strict orders and penalties is not enough to be authoritative. Those who carry out policies conducive to survival will survive even if small; those who carry out policies conducive to destruction will perish even if large.

—

A small country that actually practices culture and virtue reigns; a large country that is militaristic perishes. An army that remains whole goes to battle only after it has already won; an army doomed to defeat is one that fights first and then seeks to win.

When virtues are equal, the many prevail over the few. When powers are comparable, the intelligent prevail over the foolish.

—

When a thousand people are of like mind, they gain the power of a thousand people; when ten thousand people are of different minds, then no one is really useful. Only when commanders, soldiers, officials, and citizens operate as one body can they do battle in response to an opponent.

So, go into action after strategy has been determined; act once measures have been decided. When commanders have no dubious schemes, soldiers are not of two minds. There will be no signs of laxness in action or coarseness of speech, no tentativeness in operations. Response to opponents will be quick; deployment will be swift.

So, the people are the body of the commanders, and the commanders are the heart of the people. If the heart is true, the limbs and body follow it closely. If the heart is suspicious, the limbs and body are out of control. If the heart is not single-minded, the body does not regulate its strength. If commanders are not sincere in their need, soldiers are not brave and bold.

—

What is valued in the Way is its formlessness. Be formless, and you cannot be repressed or oppressed; you cannot be measured or figured out.

—

Those skilled at defense do not suppress anyone, and those skilled at war do not fight with anyone. As for those who understand the Way of what to prohibit and what to allow, what to open and what to close, they ride the momentum of the times and use the desire of the people to take the world.

—

When culture has but a superficial influence, power has limited effect. When virtue is liberally applied, authority's reign is extensive.

—

When people follow orders sincerely, even if small in number there is no fear. If people don't follow orders, even if large in number they are as if few.

—

When officers and soldiers are dedicated and pure, when the good are selected and the talented employed, when the right people are found to be officers, when assessments are determined and plans decided, when it is understood what would be deadly and what would foster life, when action and restraint are timely, then no opponent could fail to be startled. Therefore, a city would fall to such an attack before any war machines had been deployed; an opponent would be defeated in war before any armed clashes occurred. This is a matter of understanding the factors involved in certain victory.

So, if an army does not even skirmish unless it is sure of victory, if it does not even set out to besiege what it is not sure to take, if it fights only after the configurations of power have been determined and moves only after directives have been set out, if it masses and does not scatter ineffectively, then when it goes out it does not come back without accomplishing anything.

The only hope is that such an army does not go on the move, for if it does it will challenge the heavens and shake the earth, move the highest mountains and sweep the four seas. Ghosts and spirits will move away; birds and beasts will take flight. Against this there is no army effective in the field and no country able to defend its cities.

—

Meet the excited with calm; await the disturbed with control. Be formless, so as to master the formal; respond to change without contrivance. Then, even if you are unable to attain victory over opponents, opponents will have no way to attain victory over you.

—

When opponents go into action before you do, then you see their form. When they are excited but you are calm, then you neutralize their strength.

—

Anything that has form can be overcome; anything that takes shape can be countered. This is why sages conceal their forms in nothingness and let their minds soar in the void.

—

All creatures are susceptible to control because of their movements, so sages value stillness. If you are still, you can counter excitement; and if you hold back, you can counter initiatives.

—

The way a good general employs soldiers is to unify their minds and strengths, so the bold cannot forge ahead alone and the weak cannot retreat alone. When still, they are like a mountain; in action, they are like a storm, breaking through wherever they go, overcoming all, moving like a single body, no one able to counter and stop them. Therefore, many of the enemy are wounded, yet few soldiers actually fight.

—

Benevolence, courage, trust, and integrity are fine human qualities, but it is possible to plunder the benevolent, to incite the courageous, to deceive the trusting, and to intrigue against those with integrity. If group leaders have any of these qualities visible, they are captured by other people.

—

Only the formless are invulnerable. Sages hide in inscrutability, so their feelings cannot be observed. They operate in formlessness, so their lines cannot be crossed.

—

When the best generals use arms, they have the Way of heaven above, the advantages of earth below, and the hearts of men between; then they use them at the opportune moment, deploying them along with the momentum of the situation. This is why they have no broken troops or defeated armies.

As for mediocre generals, they do not know the Way of heaven above and do not know the advantages of earth; they only use people and momentum. Although they cannot be completely successful, their victories will be in the majority.

When it comes to inferior generals and the way they use arms, they hear a lot but confuse themselves. They know a lot but doubt themselves. They are fearful in camp and hesitant in action. Therefore, they are likely to be captured by others.

—

A good military operation has a momentum like water bursting forth from a monumental dam, like round boulders tumbling into a deep ravine. If the world sees the necessity of your military action, who will presume to battle with you?

—

The way of the warrior is to show others softness but meet them with firmness, to show others weakness but surmount them with strength, to shrink back from them but reach out to counter them.

When where you are coming from is not where you are going, and what you show is not what you plan, then no one can tell what you are doing. You are like lightning—no one can anticipate where it will strike, and it never strikes twice in the same place.

Thereby, your victories can be one hundred percent complete, in communion with hidden knowledge. When no one knows your door, this is called supreme genius.

—

What makes warriors strong is readiness to fight to the death. What makes people ready to fight to the death is justice. What makes justice possible to carry out is its awesome dignity. Therefore, when people are united by culture and equalized by martial training, they are called sure winners. When awesome dignity and justice are both exercised, this is called supreme strength.

—

In ancient times good generals always were in the vanguard themselves. They didn't set up canopies in the heat and didn't wear leather in the cold; thus they experienced the same heat and cold as their soldiers.

They did not ride over rough terrain, always dismounting when climbing hills; thus they experienced the same toil as their soldiers.

They would eat only after food had been cooked for the troops, and they would drink only after water had been drawn for the troops; thus they experienced the same hunger and thirst as their soldiers.

In battle they would stand within range of enemy fire; thus they experienced the same danger as their soldiers.

So the military operations of good generals always use accumulated gratitude to attack accumulated bitterness and accumulated love to attack accumulated hatred. Why would they not win?

—

When leaders are worthy of respect, the people are willing to work for them. When their virtue is worthy of admiration, their authority can be established.

—

Those who are skilled in the use of arms must first cultivate it in themselves before they seek it in others. They first become invincible and only then seek to prevail.

—

Generals must have three paths, four duties, five practices, and ten kinds of security.

The three paths are knowledge of heaven above, familiarity with earth below, and perception of human conditions in between.

The four duties are to secure the nation without increasing armaments, to lead without selfish interest, to face difficulty without fear of death, and to resolve doubts without trying to escape blame.

The five practices are to be flexible without being pliant, to be firm without being stiff, to be humane without being vulnerable, to be trusting yet impossible to deceive, and to have courage that cannot be overwhelmed.

The ten kinds of security are purity of spirit that cannot be clouded, far-reaching plans that cannot be stolen, firmness of integrity that cannot be changed, clarity of knowledge that cannot be obscured, not being greedy for material goods, not being addicted to anything, not being a glib talker, not pushing others to go the same way, not being easy to please, and not being easy to anger.

—

For warriors it is important that their strategy be unfathomable, in the sense that their form is concealed. The emerge unexpectedly, so that a defense cannot be prepared against them. When their strategy is visible, they have nothing left; when their form is perceptible, they are susceptible to control. Therefore, good warriors hide these in heaven above, in earth below, and among humans in between.

—

Punishment is the culmination of the use of arms. Arriving at the point where there is no punishment may be called the culmination of the culmination.

—

It is indeed painful to excise a growth, and it hurts to ingest poisonous medicines: the reason we nevertheless do these things is that they are helpful to the body. It does indeed feel good to drink water when thirsty, and it does feel comfortable to eat a big meal when hungry: the reason we nevertheless do not do these things is that they are harmful to our nature.

—

The human condition is to struggle for the greatest profit and the least loss. That is why a general does not dare to ride a white horse, and a fugitive does not dare to carry a torch by night.

—

When those who overpower the weaker meet up with equals, they fight. Victory gained by yielding, on the other hand, which comes from oneself, has immeasurable power. So it is that only sages can make many nonvictories into great victory.

—

A military leader must see and know independently. To see independently means to see what others do not see; to know independently means to know what others do not know. To see what others do not see is called perceptivity; to know what others do not know is called genius. The perceptivity of genius is what makes victory a foregone conclusion.

Those for whom victory is a foregone conclusion are those who defend what cannot be attacked and attack what cannot be defended. This is a matter of emptiness and fullness.

If there are rifts in the ranks, disaffection between commanders and officers, and the contentions they hold are not honest, the discontent builds up in the minds of the soldiers. This is called being emptied.

If the leadership is enlightened and the generals are good, then the different ranks are of like mind, and their wills are in concert.

—

When the unexpected happens, the ignorant are surprised; knowers don't think it strange.

—

Anything can be overcome except the Way. It cannot be overcome because it has no fixed form or disposition.

—

What is to be done for prosperity today, and what is to be done for justice tomorrow—this is easily said. What is to be done for justice today, and what is to be done for prosperity tomorrow—this is hardly known.

—

In human nature, nothing is more valuable than benevolence; nothing is more urgent than wisdom. Benevolence is the sustenance; wisdom is the means to put it into practice. With these two qualities as the basis, all that is beneficial is consummated with the addition of courage, strength, intelligence, quickness, diligence, cleverness, acuity, brilliance, and perspicacity.

But if one is personally undeveloped and has technical skills without benevolence and wisdom to guide them, to add all sorts of embellishments in fact increases harm. Therefore, if one has courage and daring without benevolence, one is like a madman wielding a sharp sword; if one is smart and swift without wisdom, one is as though riding on a fast mount but not knowing which way to go.

Even if one has talent and ability, if one uses them improperly and handles them inappropriately, they can only assist falsehood and dress up error. In that case it is better to have few technical skills than many.

On Peace

If you know when you have enough,
   you will not be disgraced.
If you know when to stop,
   you will not be endangered.

      —Lao-tzu, *Tao-te Ching*

Those who can maintain the world certainly do not lose their nations. Those who can maintain their nations certainly do not lose their families. Those who can take care of their families certainly do not neglect themselves. Those who can cultivate themselves certainly do not forget their minds. Those who can find the source of their minds certainly do not corrode their essential nature. Those who can completely preserve the integrity of their essential nature certainly do not waver indecisively on the Way.

Therefore, the Master of Expanded Development said, "Carefully guard within, thoroughly close without; cognizing much is defeating. Do not look, do not listen; embrace the spirit calmly, and the body will straighten itself."

None can know another without attaining it in oneself. Therefore, the *Book of Changes* says, "Close up the bag, and there is no blame or praise."

—

If you are clear, calm, and uncontrived, heaven will provide a time for you. If you are modest, frugal, and disciplined, earth will produce wealth for you.

—

When a boat is crossing a river, if an empty boat broadsides it and overturns it, the passengers in the first boat may very well be upset, but they won't be resentful.

But let there be even one person in the second boat, and suppose he doesn't respond to the calls of the passengers in the first boat, he will surely be followed by ugly voices.

The reason they are not angry in the former instance is that the boat is empty. The reason they are angry in the latter instance is that the boat is full. If you can empty yourself as a means of traveling through the world, who can criticize you?

—

Take the world lightly, and your spirit will not be burdened. Consider everything minor, and your mind will not be confused. Regard death and life as equal, and your heart will not be afraid.

—

Perfect nobility does not need a title; perfect wealth does not need possessions.

—

Those who know how to learn are like axles of a car: the center of the hub does not itself move, but with it they go a thousand miles, beginning again when they finish, operating an inexhaustible resource.

Those who do not know how to learn are as though lost: tell them the cardinal directions, and they misunderstand; listening from their own point of view, they are disoriented and therefore fail to get the gist of the whole matter.

—

Perfected people lean on a pillar that cannot be toppled, travel a road that cannot be blocked, take orders from a perennial government, and arrive wherever they go. Life cannot hang on their minds; death cannot darken their spirits.

—

When people can penetrate the deepest darkness and enter the shining light, then it is possible to talk to them about the ultimate.

—

Those in whom sense overpowers desire flourish, while those in whom desire overpowers sense perish.

—

Habitual desires deplete people's energy, likes and dislikes strain people's minds. If you don't get rid of them quickly, your will and energy will diminish day by day.

—

When you penetrate psychology, you realize that habitual desires, likes and dislikes, are external.

—

What I call happiness is when people appreciate what they have. People who appreciate what they have do not consider extravagance enjoyable and do not consider frugality a sorry state.

—

People crave position, power, and wealth, but if it is a matter of holding a map of the world in your left hand while cutting your throat with your right hand, even an ignoramus would not do that. Seen in this light, life is more valuable than worldly dominion.

—

If you know the vastness of the universe, you cannot be oppressed by death or life. If you know the harmony of nurturing life, you cannot be concerned about worldly dominion. If you know the happiness of the unborn state, you cannot be frightened by death.

—

If you are not satisfied with yourself, even if you have a whole continent for your house with all its people for your servants, this will not be enough to support you.

—

Those who can reach the point where they take no pleasure in anything find that they can now enjoy everything. Since there is nothing they do not enjoy, their happiness is supreme.

—

Those who embody the Tao are free and inexhaustible; those who rely on calculation work hard without achievement.

—

Those who rely on intelligence without the Way will surely be endangered; those who employ talent unscientifically will surely be frustrated. There are those who perish because of having many desires, but there has never been anyone imperiled by being desireless. There are those who cause disorder by their desire to govern, but no one has ever suffered loss by preservation of the constant.

—

When people have many desires, this adversely affects their sense of justice. Having many anxieties adversely affects wisdom. Having many fears adversely affects courage.

—

Limit what you keep, and you will be circumspect; minimize what you seek, and you will have what you need.

—

Clear calm is the consummation of virtue; flexible softness is the key of the Way; open selflessness and serene joyfulness enable one to make use of all things.

—

Those who want firmness must guard it with flexibility; those who want strength must preserve it with weakness.

—

If you do not contend with anyone, no one can contend with you.

—

When your spirit rules, your body benefits from obedience to it; when your body is in control, your spirit is harmed by obedience to it.

—

In completeness, it is pure simplicity; scattered, it is mixed, as though in suspension. The suspension gradually clarifies; openness is gradually filled.

It is calm as the depths of the ocean, broad as the floating clouds. It seems not to be there yet is; it seems absent yet is present.

The totality of all things goes through one opening; the roots of all affairs come from one gate. Its movement is formless; its transformations are spiritlike; its action is traceless. It always follows yet is in the lead.

—

When the spiritual light is stored in formlessness, vitality and energy return to perfect reality. Then the eyes are clear but are not used for looking; the ears are sharp but are not used for listening; the mind is expanded but is not used for thinking.

When vitality passes into the eyes, vision is clear; when it is in the ears, hearing is sharp; when it is in the mouth, speech is accurate; and when it gathers in the mind, thought is penetrating.

—

When things are done in accord with the Tao, it is not the doing of the Tao, it is the disbursal of the Tao.

—

If you seek to gain the world and forget the way of self-cultivation, you cannot even preserve your own body, much less any territory. Therefore, when order has not been stabilized while in a peaceful state, those who strive to govern will be imperiled; and when conduct has not been stabilized while there is nothing wrong in it, those in a hurry for fame will be broken.

—

What I call noncontrivance means that personal will cannot enter the public Way; likings and desires cannot warp the true arts of leadership; projects are undertaken in a reasonable manner; works are accomplished according to available resources; and you forward the spontaneous momentum of nature so that no twisted intentions can get in.

In this way things get done without anyone taking personal credit; achievements are made without anyone being known for them. This does not mean that one does not respond to sense or move when pressed.

—

No fortune is greater than having no troubles; no profit is finer than suffering no loss. What action does for people either enhances or diminishes, either fulfills or destroys, either benefits or harms. All are dangerous—perils on the way.

—

The energy of heaven is the higher soul; the energy of earth is the lower soul. Return them to the mystic chamber, so each is in its place. Keep watch over them and do not lose them; you will be connected to absolute unity above, and the vitality of absolute unity is connected to heaven.

—

The great way has no form; great kindness has no familiarity; great eloquence has no voice; great humility is not obsequious; great courage is not conceited. If you do not neglect these five things, you are getting near to the Way.

—

People can do good but cannot necessarily reap its blessings. People may avoid doing wrong but cannot necessarily avoid calamity thereby.

—

When people who are truly kind give, it is a kindness; and when they do not give, it is also a kindness. When people who are really not kind give, it is not a kindness; and when they do not give, it is also not a kindness.

—

There is real knowledge only when there are real people.

—

When people are caught up in the world, they are materially bound and spiritually drained. Therefore, they unavoidably suffer ailments from depletion.

—

The spirit is the source of knowing; when the spirit is pure, knowledge is clear. Knowing is the capital of the heart; when knowledge is objective and impartial, the heart is peaceful.

—

The spirit can rest on the tip of a hair, yet it is larger than the totality of the universe.

—

If you always want to be in emptiness, then you cannot be empty. To be empty without trying to be empty is something that is sought but cannot be brought.

—

You cannot have people tune musical instruments if they are tone deaf, and you cannot have people formulate laws if they are ignorant of the sources of order and confusion. Similarly, it is essential to have the clarity of independent perception before one can travel freely on the Way.

—

If you only look at a square inch of an ox, you won't know it's bigger than a goat; only when you see the whole body do you know how far apart they are.

—

The recalcitrant may seem knowledgeable without being knowledgeable. The dull-witted may seem humane without being humane. The impetuous may seem brave without being brave.

—

If you focus on people's shortcomings and forget about their strengths, then it will be hard to find worthy people in all the world.

—

Things depend on each other for completeness. When two people are both drowning, they cannot help each other; but when one is on dry land, then something can be done. So those who are the same cannot govern each other; this can only take place when there are differences.

—

Ostentation and deceit are born from pride. Someone who is truthful within is happy and unhurried, doing what needs to be done as naturally as a singing bird singing or a bear stretching. Who is to be proud of that?

—

Latter-day scholars do not know the unity of the Way or the sum of virtue: they pick up traces of events that have taken place and sit together talking about them. Therefore, they are learned and erudite but still have not escaped confusion.

—

A way that can be spoken of is not an eternal way; a name that can be named is not a permanent name. What can be written down or passed on to others is the dregs.

—

Put away the wine and stop the music, and the mind suddenly feels as though it has suffered a loss; it is upset, as though it has been bereft of something. What makes this happen? Using externals to amuse the internal, instead of using the internal in such a way as to make the external pleasant.

—

There are countless sights, sounds, and flavors, rarities from distant lands, oddities and curiosities that can change the aim of the mind, destabilize the vital spirit, and disturb the circulation and energy.

—

The vital spirit belongs to heaven; the physical body belongs to earth. When the vital spirit goes home and the physical body returns to its origin, where then is the self?

—

What gives life to the living never dies, though what it produces does die. What transforms things never changes, though what it transforms does change.

—

For those in prison the days are long, but for those condemned to die the days are short. The length of days has its own measure, but they seem long in one place and short in another. So there is unevenness in the heart.

—

In spring, women are thoughtful; in autumn, men are sad. They know things are changing.

—

Something that is kept inside and never divulged, something in the feelings that never sprouts—no one ever heard of this.

—

Most people can sing and cry. Once the sound is made, it enters people's ears and moves people's hearts. This is the reach of feeling.

—

Blessings come from yourself, and so do calamities. Sages do not seek praise and do not flee censure. They keep themselves upright and act honestly, so all falsehood naturally stops.

—

If you do not hide from yourself, you do not hide from others either.

—

Great people are serene, free from longing; they are calm, free from worry.

—

The spirit leaves those who make an issue of the spirit, while it abides in those who rest their spirit.

—

Calm and joyous without pride, one attains harmony.

—

When the perceptions are clear, with profound discernment free from seductive longings, and energy and will are open and calm, serenely joyful and free from habitual desires, then the internal organs are settled and full of energy that does not leak out. The vital spirit preserves the physical body inwardly and does not go outside. Then it is not difficult to see the precedents of the past and the aftermath of the future.

—

Outwardly go along with the flow, while inwardly keeping your true nature. Then your eyes and ears will not be dazzled, and your thoughts will not be confused, while the spirit within you will expand greatly to roam in the realm of absolute purity.

—

Attainment of the Tao is certain and does not depend on the flow of things. I do not let the changes of a given time determine the way I master myself.

What I call self-mastery means that my nature and life abide where they are secure.

—

When large groups attack small groups, that is considered bellicose; but when large nations annex small nations, that is considered smart. A small horse is of a kind with a large horse, but small knowledge is not of a kind with great knowledge.

—

When your reception is small, your perception is shallow. When your reception is great, your awareness is broad.

—

We may see the tip of a hair while failing to hear a peal of thunder or hear the melody of a song while failing to see a mountain. Why? A small fixation of attention results in a large measure of heedlessness.

—

People all value what they can do well and demean what they cannot do well. However, they all drown in what they value and are stymied by what they demean. What they value is what has form, and what they demean is the traceless.

—

For the sun and moon, brightness is desirable, but clouds cover them. For river waters, clarity is desirable, but sand clouds them. For human nature, balance is desirable, but habitual cravings damage it. Only sages can forget things and return to the self.

—

Clarity does not mean seeing others, just seeing oneself. Acuity does not mean hearing others, just hearing oneself. Understanding does not mean knowing others, just knowing oneself.

—

Accusing others is not as good as accusing yourself. Demanding from others is not as good as demanding from yourself.

—

When people bring up your flaws, you resent them for it; but when a mirror reflects your ugliness, you consider it a good mirror. If people can deal with others without getting the ego involved, they will avoid being dragged down.

—

The eyes, ears, and palate do not know what to take and what to leave; when the mind governs them, they each find their proper place. Seen from this point of view, it is evident that desire cannot be overcome; yet it can be done to the point where insanity does not occur, by any who master themselves and develop their nature, regulate sexual activity and moderate their dining, make their emotions gentle, and act and rest appropriately, causing this all to be in themselves.

—

Those who decorate their exterior hurt their interior; those who indulge their feelings harm their spirits; those who show their embellishments obscure their reality. Those who never forget to be crafty for even a moment inevitably stultify their nature.

—

When desires do not emerge within and perversions do not enter from without, this is called security. When there is inward and outward security, everything is moderate; everything can be accomplished.

—

Making a big deal out of doing good is like making a big deal out of doing wrong, insofar as it is not near the Way.

—

When it comes from the Way, good is unobtrusive; when it follows the Principle, skill is unsung.

—

Ideal people cultivate their conduct and cause their goodness to be unknown; they exercise generosity and cause their humanitarianism to be unnoticed.

—

Nothing in the world is easier than doing good; nothing is harder than doing evil. Here, doing good means tranquility and noncontrivance; doing evil means impetuosity and greediness.

—

When the eyes look at random, one becomes licentious. When the ears listen at random, one becomes confused. When the mouth speaks at random, one becomes disorderly. These three passageways are to be carefully guarded.

—

Success is a matter of timing, not contention. Order depends on the Tao, not on sagacity.

—

Successful people are economical in their actions and careful about time.

—

Wise people think of justice rather than profit. Immature people crave profit and ignore justice.

—

The self-confident cannot be moved by censure or praise; the contented cannot be seduced by power or profit. Therefore, those who realize the true condition of essence do not strive for what essence can do nothing about. Those who realize the true condition of destiny do not worry over what destiny can do nothing about. Those who realize the Way are not susceptible to having their harmony deranged by anything at all.

—

Those who seek much gain little. Those with large views have small knowledge.

—

There are those who seek the Tao beyond the four seas without finding it, and there are those who have it in their bodies without seeing it.

—

The Tao cannot be sought from others; it is attained in oneself. If you abandon yourself to seek from others, you are far from the Tao.

—

If you adapt to conditions and refuse excess, you will not be seduced. If you follow nature and preserve reality, there will be no change in yourself.

—

Consideration cannot overpower the course of events; action cannot overpower virtue; striving cannot overpower the Way. There is that which striving cannot accomplish; there is that which seeking cannot gain. People may reach an impasse, but the Way goes through all. Contend with the Way, and you will have bad luck.

—

When the principle of the Way goes through, human artifice dies out. Reputation and the Way are not both illustrious: if people are in love with reputation, then the Way is not employed. When the Way prevails over personality, then reputation is moot.

—

The eyes are fond of color and form, the ears are fond of voice and sound, the palate is fond of flavor: what enjoys contacts without cognizance of their profit and harm is greed. When what you eat doesn't settle in the stomach, what you listen to does not accord with the Way, and what you look at is unsuited to nature, there are battles at these three points of interaction: what uses duty to assert mastery is mind.

—

When the essential vitality is lost within, and speech and action look to externals, then one cannot avoid being a personal servant of things.

When people are ostentatious in speech and devious in action, this is because their vitality is seeking externals. Their vitality runs low and wears out, while their actions have no consummation, so mental confusion clouds their spirits, and this confusion shakes them to the roots.

The principles by which they live are inconstant, and they are outwardly infatuated with vulgarities. They bungle their decisions, while inwardly beclouding their clarity. Therefore, they hesitate all their lives and never get a moment's peace.

—

When outside and inside do not match, yet you want to make connections with things, you cover your mystic light and seek knowledge through your eyes and ears. This is giving up illumination, so the way is dark. This is called losing the Way.

—

Heaven is calm and clear; earth is stable and peaceful. Beings who lose these qualities die, while those who emulate them live.

Calm spaciousness is the house of spiritual light; open selflessness is the abode of the Tao.

Therefore, there are those who seek it outwardly and lose it inwardly; and there are those who safeguard it inwardly and gain it outwardly.

It is like the root and the branches. Draw it by the root, and all the branches and leaves cannot but follow.

—

The way of heaven and earth is enormously vast, yet it still moderates its manifestation of glory and is sparing of its spiritual light. How then could human eyes and ears work perpetually, without rest? How could the vital spirit be forever rushing around without becoming exhausted?

—

Don't be surprised; don't be startled—all things will arrange themselves. Don't cause a disturbance; don't exert pressure—all things will clarify themselves.

—

Human nature is developed by profound serenity and lightness; virtue is developed by harmonious joy and open selflessness. When externals do not confuse you inwardly, your nature finds the condition that suits it; when your nature does not disturb harmony, virtue rests in its place.

If you can get through life in the world by developing your

nature, and embrace virtue to the end of your years, it can be said that you are able to embody the Tao.

If so, there will be no thrombosis or stagnation in your blood vessels, no depressing stifled energy in your organs. Calamity and fortune will not be able to disturb you; censure and praise will not be able to affect you. Therefore, you can reach the ultimate.

—

If you are disturbed by bee stings and distracted by mosquito bites, how do you think you can be calm and empty in the face of the troubles that oppress the human mind, which are more serious than the venom of a bee sting and the annoyance of mosquito bites?

—

People change endlessly in all kinds of ways. You wear out, then are renewed. The enjoyment possible in that is incalculable.

For example, you dream you are a bird and fly through the sky; you dream you are a fish and plunge into the depths. While you are dreaming, you don't know it is a dream; after you wake up, you realize you were dreaming.

There will be a great awakening, after which you will know this present life was a dream.

When we were as yet unborn, how could we know the pleasures of life? As long as we have not died, how can we know that death is not pleasant?

—

The way has a unifying thread. When you attain the one root, it connects to a thousand branches and ten thousand leaves. This enables you to promote order when in a high position, to forget lowliness when in a low position, to enjoy work when you are poor, and to handle danger when you are at an impasse.

When there is a very cold winter, frosty and snowy, then you know the strength of the evergreens. When the situation is difficult and dangerous, with gain and loss set out before one, then you know the sage is the one who does not slip from the Way.

—

When the mind neither sorrows nor delights, that is supreme attainment of virtue. To succeed without changing is the supreme attainment of calm. To be unburdened by habitual desires is the supreme attainment of emptiness. To have no likes and dislikes is the supreme attainment of equanimity. Not getting mixed up with things is the supreme attainment of purity.

Those who can accomplish these five things reach spiritual illumination. Those who reach spiritual illumination are those who attain the inward.

Therefore, when you master the outward by means of the inward, all affairs are unspoiled.

If you can attain this within, then you can develop it outwardly.

When you attain it within, your inner organs are peaceful, and your thoughts are calm; your muscles are strong, your eyes and ears are alert and clear. You have accurate perceptions and understanding; you are firm and strong without snapping.

In a small domain you are not cramped, and in a large domain you are not careless. Your soul is not excited; your spirit is not disturbed.

Serene and aloof, you are the toughest in the world. Sensitive and responsive, when pressed you can move, infinitely calm and inscrutable.

—

Coolly sense and respond, firmly return to the root, and you sink into the Formless.

The Formless means the One. The One is that which has no match in all the world.

It stands out alone, abides solidly in solitude. Above, it penetrates the highest heavens; below, it penetrates the depths of the earth.

It is round without being put to a compass, square without being set to a ruler.

The great merges into one; the trivial piles up without root. Enveloping heaven and earth is the gateway of the Tao.

—

Pure virtue exists alone, distributed without being exhausted, used without being strained.

Therefore, when you look at it you do not see its form; when you listen for it you do not hear its sound; when you follow it you do not find its body.

It is formless, yet forms are born in it; it is soundless, yet all sounds are made in it. It is flavorless, yet all flavors are formed in it; it is colorless, yet all colors are produced in it.

So being is born from nonbeing; fulfillment emerges from emptiness.

—

Those who go first hardly know what they are getting into; those who come later find it easy to attack them. When those who go first rise to the heights, those who come later cleave to them. When those who go first descend to the depths, those who come later step on them. When those who go first suffer a fall, those who come later use it to plan. When those who go first fail in their undertakings, those who come later avoid them.

Seen in this way, those who go first are the targets of the arrows of those who come later.

—

Opportunities are changing ceaselessly. Those who get there too early have gone too far, while those who get there too late cannot catch up. As the sun and moon go through their courses, time does not go along with people. Therefore, sages do not value huge jewels as much as they value a little time. Time is hard to find and easy to lose.

—

Likes and dislikes are excesses of the mind. Habitual desires are a burden on human nature.

—

Sadness, happiness, and ill-temper make sickness accumulate. When there are many likes and dislikes, calamity follows along.

—

When the ancient sage king Yu went to a country where all the people went naked, he took off his clothes when he entered the country and put on his clothes when he left.

—

Good swimmers drown; good riders fall—both turn what they like into their misfortune.

—

Those who attain the Tao neither fear difficulty nor glory in success.

—

The *Classic of Songs* speaks of "unconsciously, unknowingly, following the law of God." To have knowledge but not contrive is to share the road with the ignorant; to have ability but not strive is to share the powers of the helpless.

That knowledge is only sensed in action when there is someone to make it known; what that ability does is only sensed when there is someone to employ it.

To have knowledge yet be as if you had none, to have ability yet be as if you had none, is correct in principle. Thereby, your successes may crown the age without that glorifying you, and your accomplishments may benefit future generations without your being known for them.

—

When there is a contest between the Way and personality, whatever makes personality prominent inhibits the Way. When personality is prominent, the Way is dormant; so danger is not far away. Therefore, when society has its big names, the day of decadence has arrived.

—

People who want to be famous will do good, and people who want to be do-gooders will initiate projects. Once it has become a business, they let go of the public and take to the private, ignore natural processes and take the responsibility on themselves.

—

The reversal of benefit and harm, the connection between calamity and disaster, should be closely examined. Sometimes when you want something, that in itself can make you lose it; and sometimes when you try to avoid something, that in itself can make you face it.

Once a man took a ride in a boat and encountered a squall. Fearful of the waves, he threw himself into the water. It was not that he did not want to live and did not fear to die, but that he was so confused by his fear of death that instead he forgot about life.

So it is with habitual desires. Once when a man stole some gold right in the middle of a bustling town, the police asked him why he took the gold right there in the open market in broad daylight, with so many people around. He said, "I only saw the gold; I didn't see the people." His heart was so set on what he wanted that he was oblivious to what he was doing.

—

Sages examine the changes of movement and rest, make the measures of receiving and giving appropriate, make feelings of like and dislike reasonable, and harmonize the degrees of joy and anger.

When movement and rest are right, no trouble is encountered. When receiving and giving are appropriate, no blame is incurred. When likes and dislikes are reasonable, no anxiety comes near. When joy and anger are in measure, no enmity invades.

Therefore, people who arrive at the Way do not take wrongful gain yet do not reject good fortune. They do not throw away what they have and do not seek what is not theirs. When one is always full, there is an overflow; when one is always empty, one is easily satisfied.

—

People who enjoy giving are invariably good at taking; people who enjoy rewards invariably have many resentments. Only those who obliterate their tracks in noncontrivance and follow the inherent nature of heaven and earth are able to master order without love of fame.

When fame is exalted, the Way does not work. When the Way is working, people have no ranks.

So, when there is praise, censure comes with it; when good appears, evil follows. Profit is the beginning of loss; fortune is the forerunner of calamity. Only those who do not seek to gain will have no loss, and only those who do not seek blessings will suffer no disasters.

—

Those who do not know the Way give up what they already have to seek what they have not yet got. They fret and worry, which leads them into being selfish and devious. Therefore, when fortune comes they rejoice, and when trouble comes they are afraid. Their spirits toil at planning and scheming; their intellects labor over their affairs. Troubles and blessings sprout and grow, but people may live their whole lives without conscience, resenting others for what they themselves have created. If they are not happy, they are anxious and have never tasted peace within; they are not masters of what they have in their hands. This is called the birth of madness.

—

Suppose three people are living in the same house, and two of them get into an argument. Each of the two arguing thinks he or she is right and will not listen to the other. The third person may be ignorant but can certainly decide who is right from the standpoint of a third party. This is not because of wisdom but because of not being involved in the argument.

—

If you increase what cannot naturally be enjoyed, and thereby diminish natural means of enjoyment, you may be so rich as to own the world and so elevated as to rule the world, but you will still be pathetic.

—

Those imbued with the Way do not lose time yet give it to others; those without the Way do lose time and take it from others.

—

In ancient times, those who preserved themselves enjoyed virtue and forgot about lowliness, so fame could not stir their ambitions. They enjoyed the Way and forgot about poverty, so profit could not stir their ambitions.

—

Human nature is generally such that it likes tranquility and dislikes anxiety; it likes leisure and dislikes toil. When the mind is always desireless, this can be called tranquility; when the body is always unoccupied, this can be called leisure.

If you set your mind free in tranquility and relinquish your body in leisure, thereby to await the direction of heaven, spontaneously happy within and free from hurry without, even the magnitude of heaven and earth cannot change you at all; even should the sun and moon be eclipsed, that does not dampen your will. Then even if you are lowly, you are as if noble; and even if you are poor, you are as if rich.

—

Enlightened people do good, but they cannot necessarily ensure fortune; they refrain from evil, but they cannot necessarily prevent calamity. When fortune occurs, it is not something they sought, so they do not take pride in their achievement. When calamity arises, it is not something they created, so they do not regret their actions.

—

When the spirit controls the body, the body obeys; when the body overrules the spirit, the spirit is exhausted. Although intelligence is useful, it needs to be returned to the spirit. This is called the great harmony.

—

Anger comes from not being angry; action comes from inaction. If you look when there is no form, you will find what can be seen. If you listen when there is no voice, you will find what can be heard.

—

The best flavor doesn't jade the palate; the best speech isn't ornate; the best amusement isn't comical; the best music isn't noisy. The master carpenter doesn't do the cutting; the master chef doesn't boil the water; the master warrior doesn't fight. Attain the Way, and virtue follows this.

—

If you consider externals important, you will be inwardly stifled by this. People chasing game do not see the mountains. When your desires are externalized, then your light is obscured.

—

Those who know themselves cannot be seduced by anything. Those who understand life and death cannot be threatened by danger.

—

What makes a shadow bend is the form that casts it; what makes an echo unclear is the voice it reflects. Those whose feelings leak out are easy to figure out inside.

—

Clear calm and serene felicity are essential human nature. Exemplars and guidelines are regulators of affairs. If you know human nature, your self-development will not be warped. If you know how affairs are regulated, your actions will not be confused.

—

To discover one point and extend it infinitely, to comprehend the whole universe in one totality—this is called consciousness. To know the branch on seeing the root, spot the target on seeing the pointing finger, hold to oneness and thus respond to multiplicity, grasp the essential and thus govern the particular—this is called art. To live by what wisdom means, go where wisdom goes, work for what wisdom holds, and act on whence wisdom proceeds— this is called the Way.

—

Once words have escaped your mouth, you can't stop them in others. Actions started nearby cannot be prevented far away.

—

When calamity occurs, people have fostered it themselves; when fortune happens, people complete it themselves. Calamity and fortune come through the same door; help and hurt are neighbors. No one but spiritually sagacious people can distinguish them.

—

If you want to abandon learning to follow nature, this is like leaving the boat and trying to walk over the water. When a fine sword first comes out of the mold, it cannot cut or pierce until it is sharpened. When a fine mirror first comes out of the mold, it cannot reflect clearly until it is ground and polished. Learning is also a way to sharpen and polish people. Those who say learning is useless are mistaken in their argument.

—

If people are born in remote lands and grow up in poverty without parents or siblings, with the result that they have never seen manners and have never heard of the ancients, and they live alone, never going out, then even if they are not naturally stupid, few of them will have any knowledge.

—

Among the inhabitants of regions where the soil is poor, there are many people of heart; this is because life is hard. Among the inhabitants of regions where the soil is rich, there are many people who are good for nothing; this is because life is easy.

—

A general philosophy for people is that attention is to be fine while will is to be great; knowledge is to be round while action is to be square; abilities are to be many while concerns are to be few.

Refinement of attention means to consider problems before they arise, to prepare against calamities before they happen, to guard against faults, and to be wary of the subtle, not daring to indulge desires.

Greatness of will means to embrace all nations, to unify different customs, to include all people as if uniting a single family, to see that judgments come together, and to be their hub.

Roundness of knowledge means to operate beginninglessly and endlessly, reaching all quarters, the deep wellspring never exhausted, responding to all things as they arise in concert.

Squareness of action means to stand up straight without unruliness, to be plain, pure, and unaffected, not to be quick to excitement in straits, and not to indulge in whims when successful.

To have many abilities means to be competent in both martial and cultural arts, mannerly in action and repose, to be able to act or refrain as is appropriate, and not to turn away from anything but to find what is ultimately right in every situation.

To have few concerns means to master skills by holding the handle, to deal with the many by attaining the essential, to govern the extensive by grasping the general, to control hyperactivity by being calm, and to work on the pivotal, using the one to unite the myriad, like the joining of the pieces of a talisman.

So, those whose attention is fine regulate the subtle; those whose will is great embrace all. Those whose knowledge is round know everything; those whose action is square refrain from doing certain things. Those whose abilities are many accomplish everything; those whose concerns are few minimize what they hold.

—

If you know all things but do not know human ways, you cannot be called wise. If you love all creatures but do not love humanity, you cannot be called benevolent. The benevolent love their kind; the wise cannot be confused.

—

The wise begin with opposition and end up with harmony. Fools begin with enjoyment and end up with sadness.

—

Usually when people think, they always consider themselves right; but when they put it into practice, what they thought was right may turn out to be wrong. This is wherein folly and wisdom differ.

—

The way of great antiquity gave life to all beings without possessiveness and developed the forms of evolution without tyranny. All creatures depended on it for life yet were unaware of its virtue; they died because of it yet could not be resentful. Those who attained it and profited thereby could not praise it; those who used it and lost out could not repudiate it.

—

When people are calm, this is their celestial nature; to act on being moved is the capacity of this nature. When the spirit responds to things that come up, this is the action of cognition; when cognition and objects come into contact, like and dislike arise.

When likes and dislikes are formalized, and cognition is lured outside, unable to return to itself, the celestial pattern is obliterated.

Therefore, those who arrive at the Tao do not replace the celestial with the human. Externally they change along with things, but internally they do not lose their true state.

On Wisdom

Sages contrive nothing,
    and so spoil nothing.
They cling to nothing,
    and so lose nothing.

—Lao-tzu, *Tao-te Ching*

Real people are those whose natures are united with the Tao. Therefore, they exist yet seem not to; they are full yet seem empty. They abide in oneness and don't know anything else; they govern themselves inwardly and do not make note of externals.

Perfectly clear, utterly plain, and without contrivance, they return to simplicity. Comprehending the fundamental and embracing the spirit, they thus roam on the edge of heaven and earth. Wandering in the vastness beyond mundane clutter, they work freely without making an issue of it.

Real people know without learning, see without looking, achieve without striving, and understand without trying. They sense and respond, act when necessary, and go when there is no choice, like the shining of light, like the emanation of rays.

—

The harmonious joyfulness and peaceful calm of ancient sages were their nature, while their deliberate attainment of practical application of the Tao was their way of life.

So it is that nature can act only in life, while life can only be clear when nature is realized.

—

Sages respond to being by nonbeing, unfailingly finding out the inner pattern; they receive fullness by emptiness, unfailingly finding out the measure. They live out their lives with calm joy and empty tranquility. Therefore, they are not too distant from anything and not too close to anything.

—

The mind is the ruler of the body, while the spirit is the treasure of the mind. When the body is worked without rest, it collapses. When the spirit is used without cease, it becomes exhausted. Sages value and respect them and do not dare to be excessive.

—

When perfected people are in a chaotic society, many of them keep their virtue, their way, and their inexhaustible wisdom hidden, finally to die without saying anything. The world does not know to value their silence.

—

When everything goes naturally, what does a sage have to do?

—

What sages learn is to return their nature to the beginning and let the mind travel freely in openness. What developed people learn is to link their nature to vast emptiness and become aware of the silent infinite.

The learning of ordinary worldlings is otherwise. They grasp at virtues and constrict their nature, inwardly worrying about their physical organs while outwardly belaboring their eyes and ears.

—

Sages send the spirit to the capital of awareness and return to the beginning of myriad things. They look at the formless and listen to the soundless. In the midst of profound darkness, they alone see light; in the midst of silent vastness, they alone have illumination.

—

Sages use the mind deliberately, based on its essence. With the support of the spirit, they finish what they begin. Therefore, their sleep is dreamless, and they awaken untroubled.

—

Blessings arise from noncontrivance; troubles arise from covetousness. Harm arises from lack of preparation; filth arises from failure to clean.

Sages do good as if they fear there is not enough of it and prepare against calamity as if they fear they cannot avoid it.

Even if you want to keep from being blinded in a cloud of dust or want to keep from getting wet as you wade across a river, you will find that you cannot do so.

Therefore, those who know themselves do not resent others; those who know their destiny do not resent heaven.

—

Those whose words are inconstant and whose acts are inconsistent are small people.

Those who observe one thing and understand one art are mediocre people.

Those with a comprehensive purview and an inclusive grasp of things, who assess abilities and employ them judiciously, are sages.

—

Sages have within them the means to contact higher potential; they do not lose their self-mastery on account of high or low status, poverty or wealth, toil or leisure.

—

Sages overcome mind; ordinary people overcome greed. Ideal people act sanely; petty people act insanely. Sanity means inward comfort with nature, outward accord with duty, reasonable action, and nonentanglement. Insanity means addiction to sensuality and emotional impulsiveness heedless of subsequent problems.

—

Insanity and sanity wound each other; greed and nature hurt each other. They cannot coexist; when one governs, the other wastes away. Therefore, sages reduce desire and follow nature.

—

Sages are not controlled by names, not governed by plans, not burdened by affairs, and not ruled by intellect. They are concealed in formlessness; their acts are traceless, and their roamings are trackless. They do not introduce fortune or start calamity; they maintain open selflessness and act when it is unavoidable.

—

Sages can be negative or positive, weak or strong. They act or remain still according to the time; they accomplish achievements based on resources. When people act, sages know what the reflections will be; when events begin, sages perceive how they will evolve.

—

With the art of the Way it is not possible to seek fame through promotion, but it is possible to develop oneself by retirement. It is not possible to gain advantages by it, but it is possible to avoid injuries.

Therefore, sages do not seek fame by their acts and do not seek praise for their wisdom. They emulate nature itself, so the ego is not involved.

—

Sages do things while they are still small and thus can overturn the great. They perceive things near at hand and thus can be mindful of things at a distance.

—

Sages are not ashamed of having low social status, but they are ashamed of not putting the Way into practice. They do not worry about their own lives being short, but they do worry about the distress of the common people.

—

When it is so clear that sages are so concerned about people, is it not contradictory to call them inactive?

—

Sages are not worried or defensive: they do not welcome what comes or send off what goes. People may be of the East, West, South, or North, but sages stand alone in the center. Therefore, they can be in the midst of a warped society without losing their straightness.

The whole world is influenced by external forces, while sages alone do not leave their sacred ground. Therefore, they do not strive to be liked and do not flee disdain, following the Way of heaven. They do not initiate and are not self-centered, according to the Principle of heaven. They do not plan ahead yet do not abandon opportunity, making a pact with heaven. They do not seek to gain yet do not reject fortune, following the example of heaven.

—

At the very beginning, people were born from nonbeing and formed of being. Once they had form, they were constrained by things. If they can go back to where they were born and be as if formless, they are called real people. Real people are never separate from the great unity.

—

Sages are inwardly concealed and do not act as initiators for others. When things come up, they manage them; and when people come to them, they respond.

—

Sages do not dress or behave ostentatiously. They wear what no one looks at, do what no one watches, and say what no one disputes. In times of ease they are not extravagant; in times of hardship they are not fearful. They do not show off when successful and are not desperate in retirement. They are different but do not seem weird; they appear ordinary, but there is no way to name them. This is called great mastery.

—

Sages emulate heaven and go along with its conditions. They are not wedded to conventional customs and are not influenced by people.

—

The practice of sages is neither to join up with anyone nor to separate from anyone.

—

Sages have no thoughts to abandon, so there is no ugliness in their minds. There is no beauty they grasp, so beauty is not lost to them. Therefore, they do not think of obtaining blessings or rewards through their religious and social activities; their purpose is to develop gratitude and respect. Only those who do not seek can have this.

—

It may be impossible to plan ahead for some events, and it may be impossible to think ahead about some things. They come up suddenly, without warning, so sages develop the Way and wait for the right time.

—

When sages do good, it is not as a means of seeking honor, yet honor follows; it is not in hopes of gain, yet gain results.

—

The beginnings of fortune and calamity are subtle, so people are heedless of them. Only sages see the beginning and know the end.

—

Sages conceal their good deeds and keep their benevolence anonymous.

—

Sages worked at various things that were different in concrete terms but united in principle and logic. They went by different roads to the same goal. In all the vicissitudes of their lives they were as of one will, never forgetting the desire to benefit people.

—

Sages do not use people for their own personal ends; they do not let their desires disturb harmony. Therefore, when they are happy, they do not rejoice too much, and when they are sad, they do not grieve too much.

—

When people desire to prosper, it is for their own sake—what benefit is it to others? When sages carry out justice, their concern comes from within—what personal profit is in it for them?

—

When sages consider human worth, all they have to do is observe a single activity. Then the worthy and the unworthy are distinguished.

—

Sages do not do acts that can be repudiated, but they do not resent it if people repudiate them. They cultivate virtue worthy of praise, but they do not seek people's praise. They cannot cause calamity not to come, but they trust themselves not to beckon it. They cannot ensure that fortune will come, but they trust themselves not to repel it. When calamity occurs, it is not that they have sought that whereby it arises; so even in extremity they are not troubled. When fortune occurs, it is not that they have sought that whereby it comes about; so even in success they are not proud. They know the control of calamity, and fortune is not up to them, so they live happily at ease, governing without contrivance.

Sages conserve what they already have and do not seek what they haven't attained. If you seek what you don't have, what you do have will be lost. If you cultivate what you already have, then what you want comes about.

Therefore, in military operations you first become invincible and then wait for vulnerability in opponents. In government you first become secure and then wait for insecurity in opponents.

—

Sages inwardly cultivate the fundamental and do not outwardly adorn the secondary; they preserve their vital spirit, laying their cunning to rest. They are free and do nothing, yet there is nothing they do not do; they are aloof and govern nothing, yet there is nothing they do not govern.

That they do nothing means they do not act before others; that there is nothing they do not do means they go by what others do. That they govern nothing means they do not change what happens naturally; that there is nothing they do not govern means they go by what is appropriate for others.

All things have their outcomes, but only sages know how to keep to the root; all events have their implications, but only sages know to keep by the gate. Therefore, they fathom the fathomless and reach the end of the endless. They notice things without being blinded; they respond like echoes without wearing out. This is called celestial understanding.

Therefore, those who attain the Tao are weak in ambition but strong in works; their hearts are open and their responses appropriate.

—

Sages do not need authority to be noble, do not need wealth to be rich, and do not need power to be strong. Peaceful and empty, they are not subject to outside influences; they fly freely with evolution.

Thus they leave gold hidden in the mountains; they leave pearls hidden in the sea. They do not see profit in material possessions; they do not covet power and fame.

They do not take pleasure in ease; they are not saddened in straits. They do not find comfort in high social status; they do not find peril in low social status. Their body, mind, energy, and will each rests in its proper place.

The body is the house of life; energy is the basis of life; mind is the regulator of life. When one of these loses its place, the other two suffer.

Sages teach people to keep the body, energy, and mind in their places so that they carry out their functions without mutual interference.

The body is ruined if it is kept in a situation that is not comfortable. Energy is drained if it is used in a way that is not conducive to fulfillment. The mind becomes dim if it is used in a way that is not appropriate. It is imperative to be wary of these three things.

—

The reason one does not wear a leather coat in summer is not to spare the coat but because it is too warm. The reason one does not use a fan in winter is not disdain for fans but because it is too cool.

Sages eat according to the size of their bellies and dress according to the size of their bodies, adjusting to the needs and no more—so how could a mind defiled by greed arise in them?

Therefore, those who are capable of leading the world are those who have no ambition to use the world; those who are capable of sustaining fame are those who do nothing excessive to seek it.

—

When you truly understand human nature and destiny, kindness and justice are naturally included. Ups and downs cannot disturb your mind.

When nothing covers the spirit and nothing burdens the mind, you experience penetrating clarity and expansive outreach. Serene, without preoccupation, not fixated on anything, dealing with everything calmly, you are not susceptible to corruption by sensuality.

Rhetoric cannot sway you; beauty cannot influence you. Intellectuals cannot move you; powermongers cannot frighten you. This is the freedom of real people.